WORLD WAR II:

EUROPE

Reg Grant

WORLD ALMANAC® LIBRARY

Please visit our web site at: www.worldalmanaclibrary.com
For a free color catalog describing World Almanac® Library's list of high-quality books
and multimedia programs, call 1-800-848-2928 (USA) or 1-800-387-3178 (Canada).
World Almanac® Library's fax: (414) 332-3567.

Library of Congress Cataloging-in-Publication Data

Grant, Reg G.
    World War II: Europe / by Reg Grant.
        p. cm. — (Atlas of conflicts)
    Includes bibliographical references and index.
    ISBN 0-8368-5669-4 (lib. bdg.)
    ISBN 0-8368-5676-7 (softcover)
    1. World War, 1939-1945—Campaigns—Europe—Juvenile literature. [1. World War, 1939-1945—
Campaigns—Europe—Maps for children.] I. Title. II. Series.
    D743.G644   2004
    940.54'21—dc22
                                                            2004046471

This North American edition first published in 2005 by
World Almanac® Library
330 West Olive Street, Suite 100
Milwaukee, WI 53212 USA

This U.S. edition copyright © 2005 by World Almanac® Library.
Original edition copyright © 2004 by Arcturus Publishing Limited.
Additional end matter copyright © 2005 by World Almanac® Library.

Produced by Arcturus Publishing Limited.
Series concept: Alex Woolf
Editor: Philip de Ste. Croix
Designer: Simon Burrough
Cartography: The Map Studio
Consultant: Paul Cornish, Imperial War Museum, London
Picture researcher: Thomas Mitchell

World Almanac® Library editor: Gini Holland
World Almanac® Library design: Steve Schraenkler
World Almanac® Library production: Jessica Morris

All the photographs in this book were supplied by Getty Images
and are reproduced here with permission.

Printed in Italy

1 2 3 4 5 6 7 8 9 08 07 06 05 04

CONTENTS

CHAPTER 1
THE WAR BEGINS

German dictator Adolf Hitler shakes hands with army officers at a Nazi Party rally in 1934. Hitler rapidly expanded Germany's armed forces through the 1930s.

World War II is generally said to have started on September 1, 1939, when Germany, ruled by the Nazi dictator Adolf Hitler, invaded its neighbor Poland. Conflict in Europe, however, had actually been building up for several years before that date.

Hitler came to power in Germany in 1933. He had publicly committed himself to the overthrow of the Versailles Treaty, the peace treaty imposed by the victors on a defeated Germany in 1919 at the end of the Great War (now known as World War I). Under the terms of this treaty, which had been designed to keep

Germany from starting another world war, Germany was only allowed a small army with limited armaments and no air force. It was not allowed to have troops in its own Rhineland, which bordered France. The borders of Germany set by the treaty left many German-speaking people outside the country's borders. Austria, which was mostly German-speaking, was forbidden to become part of Germany.

Hitler challenged the Versailles settlement step by step. He rapidly set about rebuilding Germany's armed forces, including its air force. Rearmament was already well under way by the time it was officially announced in 1935. The following year, German troops marched into the demilitarized Rhineland. Britain and France, the two powers mainly responsible for the Versailles Treaty (and with a major interest in upholding it to keep Germany contained) protested but did nothing.

THE AXIS ALLIANCE World War II would soon become a struggle between Hitler's Axis Alliance and the Allies of Britain. In 1936, Hitler formed the Axis alliance with another dictator, Italy's Benito Mussolini, who had angered Britain and France in 1935 by invading the independent African country of Abyssinia (now Ethiopia). When civil war broke out in Spain in July 1936, Germany and Italy sent forces to support General Francisco Franco's Nationalist rebels against the Republican government. Franco triumphed in 1939 and became Spain's dictator.

Meanwhile, in March 1938, encouraged by his success in remilitarizing the Rhineland, Hitler annexed Austria. This was known as the *Anschluss* ("joining together"). Hitler's army faced no resistance, and he was greeted by cheering crowds in the Austrian capital, Vienna. Again, Britain and France did nothing.

Next, Hitler's attention turned to Czechoslovakia, a well-armed, democratic ally of France. Hitler threatened to invade Czechoslovakia to "liberate" the Germans living in Czechoslovakia's Sudetenland area. This seemed certain to lead to war with Britain and France. Instead, at a Munich conference in September 1938, Britain and France joined Germany and Italy and ordered the Czechs to hand over Sudetenland to Germany. British prime minister Neville Chamberlain

	Germany
	Saarland, incorporated 1935
	Rhineland, remilitarized 1936
–·–·–	International boundary, 1937
	Austria, annexed by Germany, March 1938
	Sudetenland, annexed by Germany, September 1938
	To Hungary, November 1938
	Bohemia & Moravia, annexed to Germany, March 1939
	Slovakia, as a client state of Nazi Germany, nominally independent from September 1938

0   200 miles
0   200 kilometers

HITLER'S ACHIEVEMENTS

In April 1939, German Nazi dictator Adolf Hitler looked back triumphantly over his successes. He declared: *"I have . . . endeavoured to destroy sheet by sheet that Treaty [of Versailles] which . . . contains the vilest oppression which peoples and human beings have ever been expected to put up with. I have brought back to the Reich provinces stolen from us in 1919; I have led back to their native country millions of Germans who were torn away from us and were in misery . . ."*

—Quoted in *Hitler*, Joachim Fest

Above: The Saarland voted to rejoin Germany in 1935. The rest of Germany's expansion was achieved by the threat of military action.

Right: Hitler drives triumphantly through the streets of the Austrian capital, Vienna, after the annexation of Austria—the *Anschluss*—in June 1938.

Danzig—now Gdansk—on the Baltic provided Hitler with a pretext for invading Poland in September 1939. Once the Soviet Union invaded from the east, the Poles had no chance. Germany and the Soviet Union had secretly agreed to partition Poland between themselves before the war began.

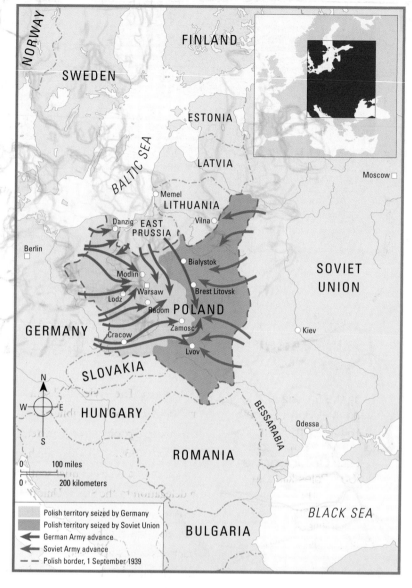

returned to Britain claiming "peace with honor," for allowing German forces to occupy the Sudetenland without a shot being fired.

Chamberlain and other "appeasers" believed that if Hitler was allowed to overturn the Versailles Treaty, gathering all German-speaking people within Germany's borders, he would be satisfied and peace would be maintained. In reality, Hitler's ambitions went much further. His ultimate goal, as he told his generals in 1939, was to obtain "living space (*Lebensraum*) in the East." This meant that Germany must conquer Slav peoples such as the Czechs, Poles, and Russians to create a German-ruled empire that would dominate Europe. This would also allow Hitler to crush other groups he hated and feared, especially communists and Jews.

Hitler had declared the Sudetenland his "last territorial claim in Europe." Instead, in March 1939, German troops marched into the Czech capital, Prague, and Czechoslovakia ceased to exist. In the same month, Germany took over Memel, Lithuania, on the Baltic, and Italy invaded Albania. Then the focus shifted to Poland, which disputed the port of Danzig (Gdansk) with Germany. Although it had a mainly German population, the peace treaty had made Danzig a "Free City" linked to Poland. Hitler demanded that Danzig be returned to Germany and that a "corridor" through Poland link Germany with East Prussia.

THE SOVIET ALLIANCE

In April 1939, shamed by their failure to defend Czechoslovakia, Britain and France signed a treaty with Poland, committing themselves to go to war if the Poles were attacked. The crucial issue then was the position of the Soviet Union, led by the communist dictator Josef Stalin. The British, French, and Polish democracies disliked and distrusted Stalin. In the summer of 1939, however, Britain and France sought an alliance with the Soviet Union, aware that only the Soviets were in a geographical position to give the Poles immediate military assistance in case of a German invasion.

To the world, Hitler and Stalin appeared to be enemies. Nazism was an explicitly anti-communist

Above: German soldiers pull down a barrier on the Polish border on September 1, 1939. Two days later, in response to the invasion of Poland, Britain and France declared war on Germany.

DEVASTATING DEFEAT

During the fighting in Poland in 1939, the death toll was high and many more were taken prisoner. The estimated figures are:

60,000	Poles killed in action
25,000	Polish civilians killed
694,000	Polish prisoners in German hands
217,000	Polish prisoners in Soviet hands

German losses, although substantial, were far lighter:

14,000	German soldiers killed

movement. The Soviets had sent military aid to the Republican side in the Spanish Civil War. Yet, in August 1939, while the British and French dithered, Hitler sent a delegation to the Soviet Union that struck a ruthless deal with the Soviets. Publicly, this Nazi-Soviet Pact was a non-aggression treaty, saying that Nazi Germany and the Soviet Union would not attack one another. In fact, the two powers secretly agreed to partition Poland between them.

German troops invaded Poland on September 1, 1939. Poland had a large army, but its equipment was out-of-date. Germany, by contrast, used its most modern tank formations and aircraft in the invasion. The tanks moved fast, punching holes in the Polish lines and penetrating deep inside Poland. German tanks were supported by. Stuka dive-bombers acting as "aerial artillery." The German *Luftwaffe* (air force) also bombed Polish cities, terrorizing the population.

The Polish forces were already in disarray when, on September 17, the Soviet Union invaded eastern Poland. The Polish government

Soviet commisar for foreign affairs Vyacheslav Molotov signs a non-aggression pact with Nazi Germany on August 23, 1939, as German foreign minister Joachim von Ribbentrop (left) looks on.

7

fled the country the next day. Warsaw, Poland's capital, surrendered on September 28. The defeat of Poland had taken four weeks.

WAR ON GERMANY

The German invasion of Poland forced Britain and France to declare war on Germany on September 3. The British and French government, however, still recovering from the trauma of World War I, had little enthusiasm for war and did nothing effective to help the Poles. While it could have attacked its neighbor Germany, France was committed to a defensive strategy. A British Expeditionary Force was sent to France, but these Allied forces stayed on the defensive—even though, with the best German troops occupied in Poland, Germany's western border would have been vulnerable to a swift attack. Once Germany defeated Poland, Britain and France felt even less inclined to attack.

Finnish soldiers wearing winter camouflage man a machine gun during the war between Finland and the Soviet Union in 1939-40.

Below: The Finns used troops on skis to launch counteroffensives after the Soviet invasion.

Germany and the Soviet Union duly carved up Poland between them. The Soviet Union also bullied the independent Baltic states, Estonia, Latvia, and Lithuania, into allowing Soviet troops to be stationed in their territory. Another of the Soviet Union's neighbors, Finland, was not as accommodating.

The Soviet Union proposed changes to its border with Finland that would have improved the Soviet defensive position in case of an attack from the west. The Finns refused. On November 30, 1939, the Soviet Red Army invaded Finland. To their surprise, they met fierce resistance. In harsh winter weather, over 120,000 Soviet soldiers died attempting to breach the Finnish defenses. As Finnish resistance held the Soviet army at bay, Britain and France discussed sending an expeditionary force to support the Finns—an action that would have put them simultaneously at war with the Soviet Union and Germany.

In February 1940, however, the Soviet Red Army broke through, and the following month the Finns were forced to accept a peace agreement that gave the Soviet Union even more territory than it had originally requested. In the summer of 1940, Stalin went on to absorb Estonia, Latvia, and Lithuania into the Soviet Union and took the province of Bessarabia from Romania. By then, however, momentous events in Western Europe had distracted attention from these Eastern European concerns.

INCAPABLE REDS

The events of the "Winter War" led many people to underestimate Soviet military strength. In a radio broadcast in January 1940, Winston Churchill, then Britain's First Lord of the Admiralty, said that Finland *"had exposed, for the world to see, the incapacity of the Red Army."*
—Quoted in *History of the Second World War*, B.H. Liddel Hart

The Mannerheim Line, a strong defensive position named after Finland's senior military commander, was key to the war between the Soviet Union and Finland in 1939–40. After the Soviets broke through the Line in February 1940, the Finns had to agree to a negotiated peace.

CHAPTER 2:
BLITZKRIEG

Above: The Junkers Ju-87 dive-bomber, known as the *Stuka*, was a crucial weapon in Germany's *"Blitzkrieg"* offensives in the early years of the war.

The period between September 1939 and April 1940 in western Europe was dubbed the "Phony War." The British Expeditionary Force (BEF) in France numbered more than 350,000 troops by spring 1940, and France had mobilized an army almost five million strong. Still, there was no significant fighting. Allied forces passively awaited a German offensive, manning the Maginot Line (*see map on page 5*), a powerful concrete fortification that France had built along its own and neutral Belgium's borders to protect them from another German invasion after World War I.

In April 1940, partly in response to criticism of their lack of military action, Britain and France decided to cut off supplies of iron ore that were being exported to Germany from mines in neutral Sweden. The iron ore was being shipped chiefly through Narvik, a port in another neutral country, Norway. On April 8, the Allies sent ships to mine Norwegian coastal waters with explosives. They also prepared to land troops at key Norwegian ports.

GERMANY ATTACKS NORWAY

Germany had been planning its own invasion of Norway. On April 9, German troops seized control of neutral Denmark and moved on to attack Norway. In a series of lightning moves, they occupied coastal

German troops drag a gun up a beach during the Norwegian campaign in the spring of 1940.

towns from Oslo in the south to Narvik in the far north. Airborne troops were parachuted in to capture key airfields—the first use of parachutists in war—but most of the German soldiers arrived by ship.

THE ROYAL NAVY The British Royal Navy was unable to stop German ships from delivering and then resupplying troops, because the British warships could not operate effectively while within range of German land-based aircraft. The Royal Navy succeeded in sinking a fair number of German warships,

especially in fierce battles at Narvik, but most of Norway was in German hands by early May 1940.

In Britain, the defeat in Norway undermined confidence in Chamberlain's leadership. Therefore, on May 10, Winston Churchill replaced Chamberlain as prime minister. On Churchill's first day as prime minister, the Germans launched their long-feared offensive on the western front.

The German army was easily outnumbered by British and French troops. While Germany had fewer tanks, however, it had more aircraft than its opponents,

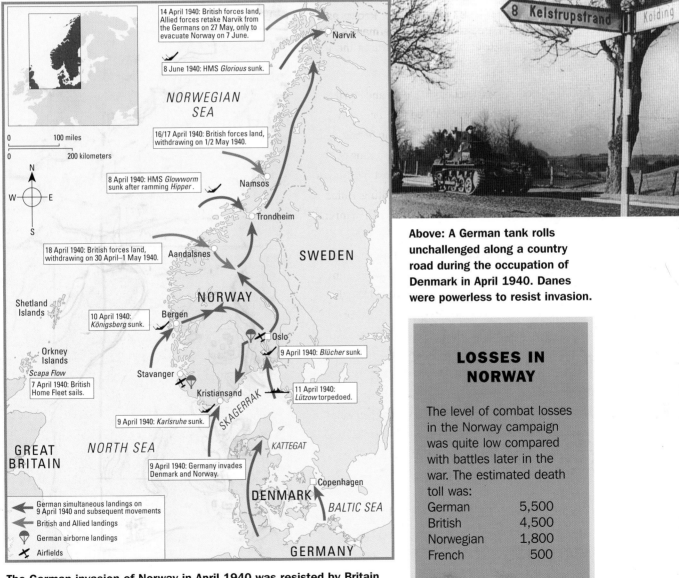

14 April 1940: British forces land, Allied forces retake Narvik from the Germans on 27 May, only to evacuate Norway on 7 June.

8 June 1940: HMS *Glorious* sunk.

16/17 April 1940: British forces land, withdrawing on 1/2 May 1940.

8 April 1940: HMS *Glowworm* sunk after ramming *Hipper*.

18 April 1940: British forces land, withdrawing on 30 April–1 May 1940.

10 April 1940: *Königsberg* sunk.

7 April 1940: British Home Fleet sails.

9 April 1940: *Blücher* sunk.

11 April 1940: *Lützow* torpedoed.

9 April 1940: *Karlsruhe* sunk.

9 April 1940: Germany invades Denmark and Norway.

NORWEGIAN SEA

0   100 miles
0   200 kilometers

N
W   E
S

Narvik

Namsos

Trondheim

Aandalsnes

SWEDEN

NORWAY

Bergen

Oslo

Shetland Islands

Orkney Islands
Scapa Flow

Stavanger

Kristiansand

SKAGERRAK

GREAT BRITAIN

NORTH SEA

KATTEGAT

Copenhagen

DENMARK

BALTIC SEA

GERMANY

German simultaneous landings on 9 April 1940 and subsequent movements
British and Allied landings
German airborne landings
Airfields

The German invasion of Norway in April 1940 was resisted by Britain and France, who also sent ships and landed troops.

Above: A German tank rolls unchallenged along a country road during the occupation of Denmark in April 1940. Danes were powerless to resist invasion.

LOSSES IN NORWAY

The level of combat losses in the Norway campaign was quite low compared with battles later in the war. The estimated death toll was:

German	5,500
British	4,500
Norwegian	1,800
French	500

so Germany triumphed with the "*Blitzkrieg*" (lightning war) tactics first employed against Poland—fast-moving armored columns that broke through or outflanked enemy defenses, backed by armed aircraft that caused panic and terror behind the lines.

Germany began its offensive by invading Belgium and the Netherlands, both neutral countries. In a series of surprise attacks, Germany's airborne troops seized bridges, airfields, and the key Belgian fortress of Eben Emael, allowing armored forces to quickly penetrate deep into enemy territory. Within five days, the Netherlands surrendered, but not before German bombers devastated their port city of Rotterdam. Meanwhile, the best elements of the British and French armies advanced into Belgium to meet the advancing Germans. This was a fatal mistake.

The Germans had originally planned to launch their main thrust through northern Belgium. Instead, during the winter of 1939–40, Hitler adopted a plan proposed by General Erich von Manstein. This called for a major attack by armored divisions much further south, through the Ardennes region. Since the Ardennes was rough, wooded country, considered almost impassable, Allied defenses in this sector were weak. Commanded by General Heinz Guderian, the spearhead of the German *panzers* (armored vehicles) crossed the Meuse River near Sedan, France, on May 13, 1940. They broke through the Allied lines and sped northwest toward the English Channel coast, which they reached on May 20. The Allied forces in Belgium were cut off from behind.

The only option open to the trapped BEF and its Allies inside Belgium was escape by sea. Fortunately for the Allies, the German armor had temporarily halted its advance on May 23, leaving the Channel port of Dunkirk, France, still in Allied hands. Between May 26 and June 3, under constant bombardment, about 338,000 men were evacuated from the port and beaches of Dunkirk. Most escaped on Royal Navy or merchant navy vessels, but a fleet of civilians in fishing boats, yachts, tugs, and barges rushed across the English Channel, heroically rescuing thousands of troops and ferrying them back to England.

CHURCHILL DEFIANT

On June 4, 1940, Prime Minister Winston Churchill told the House of Commons: *"We shall defend our island, whatever the cost may be, we shall fight on the beaches, we shall fight on the landing grounds, we shall fight in the fields and in the streets, we shall fight in the hills; we shall never surrender."*

—Quoted in *The Most Dangerous Enemy: A History of Battle of Britain*, S. Bungay

Allied troops wait to be evacuated from the beach at Dunkirk. Men formed lines into the sea, where small boats took them on board.

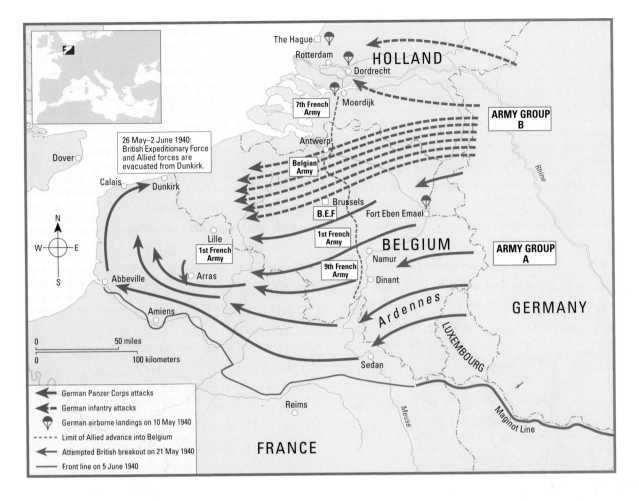

26 May–2 June 1940:
British Expeditionary Force
and Allied forces are
evacuated from Dunkirk.

German Panzer Corps attacks

German infantry attacks

German airborne landings on 10 May 1940

Limit of Allied advance into Belgium

Attempted British breakout on 21 May 1940

Front line on 5 June 1940

Dunkirk was a huge escape, but the scale and speed of the German victory was more astonishing. On June 5, the Germans resumed their offensive, driving south and west into France and sweeping the French army aside. On June 14 the Germans entered Paris. Two days later a new French government, headed by Marshal Philippe Pétain, asked for an armistice. The fighting stopped on June 25, 1940. Germany occupied northern and western France, while Pétain collaborated with Germany to govern the south from the town of Vichy.

Although Britain had brought most of its soldiers back safely from Dunkirk, they lost almost all their tanks, artillery, and other heavy equipment. Hitler hoped that Britain, like France, would accept defeat and ask for peace terms, as some British government officials wanted. But Churchill was determined to fight on. On July 16, realizing that the British would not make peace, Hitler ordered his generals to prepare an invasion of Britain, Operation Sea Lion. He also ordered an air offensive. The goal of the *Luftwaffe*,

Above: The breakthrough of German p*anzers* at Sedan, France, and their rapid progress to the English Channel coast cut off the Allied armies that had advanced into Belgium. Blocked on three sides, Dunkirk, France, provided their only escape route.

German tanks advance through Belgium in May 1940. The German army used *panzer* formations as a shock-attack force, creating a new form of mobile warfare.

A *Luftwaffe*
**Messerschmitt
Me-110 is shot down
over southern
England during the
Battle of Britain.
Often glamorized
since, the air battle
was in fact a tough
war of attrition, or
the gradual wearing
down and destruction
of enemy forces.**

Proposed German landings for Operation Sea Lion
German bridgehead for Operation Sea Lion
Proposed German airborne landing
German bomber base
German fighter base
British fighter base

Glasgow

LUFTFLOTTE 5
(from Norway
and Denmark)

Newcastle

FIGHTER COMMAND
GROUP 13

Hull

NORTH SEA

Liverpool   Manchester

Nottingham

FIGHTER COMMAND
GROUP 12

Birmingham

Coventry

Swansea

Cardiff

Bristol

London

FIGHTER
COMMAND
GROUP 11

Ramsgate

Folkestone   Dover

Calais

FIGHTER COMMAND
GROUP 10

Southampton

Brighton

Boulogne

**ARMY GROUP
A**

LUFTFLOTTE 2

Ventnor

Plymouth

ENGLISH CHANNEL

Cherbourg

**ARMY GROUP
B**

LUFTFLOTTE 3

0   50 miles
0   50 kilometers

N
W — E
S

**Above: Operation Sea Lion, the planned German invasion of
Britain in summer 1940, never took place. Instead a battle for
command of the air—the Battle of Britain—raged, mostly over
southern England.**

—already clashing with the Royal Air Force (RAF) over control of
the English Channel—was to "overcome the British air force with
all means at its disposal and in the shortest possible time."

The *Luftwaffe's* attempt to establish air superiority is known as
the Battle of Britain. Operating from airfields in occupied France,
the Germans were only a few minutes flying time from southern
England. Britain's air defenses were, however, some of the best
organized in the world. Radar stations and ground observers
radioed warning of approaching enemy planes to operations
rooms. They in turn alerted airfields to scramble RAF Hurricanes

THE BATTLE OF BRITAIN

The *Luftwaffe's* overall losses in the Battle of Britain were far higher than the RAF's, even though the RAF lost more planes. More Germans died because many of their bombers carried a crew of four.

Luftwaffe losses:
1,887 aircraft, of which 873 were fighters; 2,698 airmen

RAF Fighter Command losses:
1,023 aircraft; 544 airmen

RAF fighter pilots run to their aircraft to meet an attack. Every second counted, because pilots had to gain sufficient altitude before meeting the enemy.

and Spitfires Fighter Command. Flown by Canadians, New Zealanders, South Africans, Australians, Poles, and Czechs as well as British pilots, some of these fighters engaged the German *Messerschmitts* in "dogfights" while others took on the German bombers.

THE BLITZ From mid-August through the first week in September 1940, the *Luftwaffe* repeatedly attacked airfields, aircraft factories, and radar installations in an attempt to wear down RAF resistance. Yet, led by Sir Hugh Dowding, RAF Fighter Command managed its resources well, steadily inflicting damage on the *Luftwaffe* while minimizing its own losses. On September 7, the *Luftwaffe* switched to bombing London, England. Mass daylight raids led to some major air battles—almost 1,000 German aircraft were involved on September 15—but they did not bring the *Luftwaffe* any closer to achieving command of the air. By October, Germany had abandoned its plans for invading Britain and the *Luftwaffe* concentrated on bombing Britain's cities by night.

Dubbed "the Blitz," the intensive night bombing campaign lasted from September 1940 to May 1941. Although London was the main target, many other British cities were hit, including Liverpool, Coventry, Bristol, Plymouth, Belfast, and Cardiff. At first, air defenses were almost powerless against night attacks and the bombers met little resistance. Only gradually did the development of radar-guided night fighters and antiaircraft guns begin to allow the defenders to hit back. Bombing was a terrifying experience for the civilian population—some 43,000 people were killed in the Blitz. It failed, however, either to destroy Britain's industries or frighten the British into surrender.

It has often been said that during this period Britain "stood alone," but this was never altogether true. Britain had the support of its Commonwealth and also, increasingly, of the United States. When war broke out in Europe, most U.S. citizens strongly opposed getting involved in the conflict. The spectacle of the Battle of Britain and the Blitz, however, helped swing U.S. opinion behind Britain. This was of great help to U.S. President Franklin D. Roosevelt, who was personally

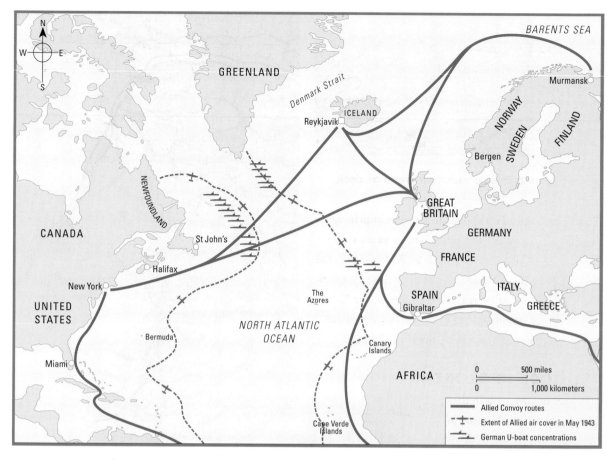

convinced that the survival of Britain was essential to the defense of the United States.

Roosevelt at first hoped to keep the United States out of the fighting by giving Britain the tools to do the job—the U.S. would be "the arsenal of democracy." Under the Lend-Lease program, approved by the U.S. Congress in March 1941, the United States provided Britain with arms without immediate payment. The program was later extended to other allies of the United States, including the Soviet Union.

THE BATTLE OF THE ATLANTIC

The only way to get U.S.-manufactured armaments and other supplies to Britain was by ship. This led to the Battle of the Atlantic—a long struggle against German surface raiders and, above all, U-boats

Above: The Allied supply lines across the Atlantic from the U.S. and Canada to Britain, and north to the Soviet port of Murmansk, were crucial to Britain's survival.

President Roosevelt (left) and Prime Minister Churchill meet on a warship in August 1941. This led to an Anglo-American declaration of principles, the Atlantic Charter.

(German submarines) that sought to cut Britain's ocean supply line. Through 1941, the United States was drawn into this conflict at sea step-by-step. By the second half of the year, without being officially at war with Germany, U.S. naval vessels were escorting merchant convoys part way across the Atlantic.

In August 1941, Churchill and Roosevelt met on board a warship off the Newfoundland coast of

German U-boats line up with their crews on deck.

Canada and agreed on a joint declaration of principles, the Atlantic Charter. The United States was thus already thoroughly committed to the British side in the war when Germany's Asian ally Japan attacked the U.S. Pacific naval base at Pearl Harbor on December 7, 1941. Hitler then put an end to any further American hesitations by declaring war on the United States.

THE CODE IS BROKEN

Still, U.S. involvement in the European war would come to nothing if the Allies could not ship men and equipment across the Atlantic. In 1942, U-boat "wolf packs" sank 7.8 million tons of Allied shipping. In fact, the Allies were losing more ships than they could build. If this had continued, Britain might have had to surrender for lack of food, fuel, and other essential supplies.

In 1943, however, the situation was transformed by a combination of factors, especially long-range aircraft used on anti-submarine patrols and British codebreakers who cracked German naval codes. Almost 100 U-boats—a quarter of the entire German submarine force—were destroyed in the first five months of the year. They never again threatened to cut the link between the U.S. and Europe.

IT MUST BE DONE

In May 1941, although the United States was not yet at war with Germany, U.S. President Franklin D. Roosevelt told the American people: *"The delivery of needed supplies to Britain is imperative. This can be done. It must be done. It will be done."*

—Quoted in *The Second World War*, Martin Gilbert

The crew of an Atlantic convoy escort vessel watch a depth charge explode. Depth charges were used to attack submerged U-boats.

CHAPTER 3
WAR IN THE MEDITERRANEAN

Swordfish biplanes fly over HMS *Illustrious*. Swordfish from the *Illustrious* devastated the Italian fleet at Taranto in November 1940.

Despite his Axis alliance with Nazi Germany, Italian dictator Benito Mussolini did not go to war in September 1939. He was only too aware of the weaknesses of his armed forces. Instead, he waited until a German victory seemed assured, declaring war on Britain and France on June 10, 1940. He hoped to exploit this opportunity to extend Italy's empire in North and East Africa and take effective control of the Mediterranean at little military cost to Italy.

Britain's position in the Mediterranean looked difficult in the summer of 1940. There were British bases at Gibraltar, Spain, and on the island of Malta, south of Sicily. British troops were also stationed in Egypt to defend the Suez Canal, a key communications link with the British Commonwealth, and in Palestine and Cyprus. Most of the rest of the Mediterranean was in hostile hands. Italy controlled Libya in North Africa and some of the Greek islands. Spain under General Franco was neutral but but friendly with Hitler and

Mussolini. The French government at Vichy controlled southern France and collaborated with Nazi Germany to help them carry out their racist and political goals. Britain had hopes that the French colonial authorities ruling Syria, Lebanon, and French North Africa would side with General Charles de Gaulle's Free French movement, which fought alongside the British. Instead, they stayed loyal to Vichy. Vichy France's hostility to Britain was strengthened in July 1940, when the Royal Navy sank French warships in the Algerian port of Mers-el-Kébir to keep them from falling into the hands of the Germans.

THE ITALIANS IN AFRICA While Britain's position in the Mediterranean appeared weak, it was in fact Italy that at first suffered disaster after disaster. In North Africa, the Italian army advanced into Egypt only to be trounced by a far smaller British and Commonwealth force, which then pushed deep into

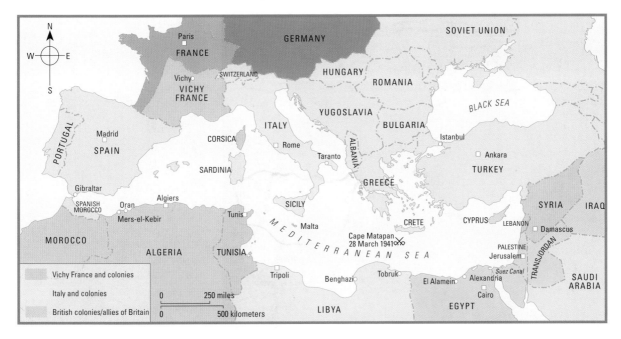

In 1940, much of the Mediterranean zone was in the hands of powers hostile to Britain—Vichy France and Italy. Malta was a key staging post for the British navy between Gibraltar and Egypt.

Libya, taking 130,000 Italian prisoners. Further south, Britain evicted Italy from its recently won colony of Abyssinia (now Ethiopia). In November 1940, Swordfish biplanes from the Royal Navy aircraft carrier HMS *Illustrious* crippled three battleships and a cruiser in a daring raid on the Italian port of Taranto. The Italian navy took another battering in an encounter with the British fleet at Cape Matapan, Greece, five months later. A further setback for Mussolini came in Greece, where an Italian invasion in October 1940 stalled in the face of stiff Greek resistance.

Italy's weakness forced Germany to send aid. German forces arrived in the Mediterranean theater and quickly turned the situation around. *Luftwaffe* units,

Italian soldiers who have surrendered to the British prepare a meal in a prisoner-of-war camp in Libya, North Africa. The Italian troops were generally poorly trained, badly led, and lacked up-to-date equipment.

Above: Italy invaded Greece in October 1940 but the Greeks drove the invaders back into Albania. Britain sent troops to aid the Greeks, but in April 1941 the Germans quickly overran both Yugoslavia and Greece. Most of the British forces withdrew to Crete, which then also fell to Germany.

German parachute troops led the invasion of Crete in May 1941. The paratroopers suffered heavy losses but were able to seize a vital airfield.

stationed in Sicily from the start of 1941, brought Malta under heavy aerial bombardment and inflicted severe punishment on British naval and merchant ships. In North Africa, German General Erwin Rommel and his *Afrika Korps* troops arrived in Tripoli in February 1941 and swiftly drove the British back out of Libya (*see map on page 23*).

One reason for Rommel's instant success was that some 60,000 British, New Zealander, and Australian troops had been transferred from North Africa to Greece, in anticipation of German intervention there in support of the Italians. Before the Germans could invade Greece, however, another crisis erupted in the region. In Yugoslavia, an uprising in late March 1941 overthrew the pro-German government and replaced it with a pro-British regime. Hitler immediately decided to invade Yugoslavia as well as Greece.

YUGOSLAVIA CONQUERED

Beginning on April 6, 1941, the Germans, aided by Italian and Hungarian troops, carried out another astonishingly swift and effective campaign, routing their enemies in just three weeks. Yugoslavia was conquered and broken up, the largest single part becoming the state of Croatia, closely tied to Italy and Germany. Greece was also overrun. Some 50,000 British, Commonwealth, and Greek soldiers were evacuated from southern Greece by sea, most of them being taken to the Greek island of Crete.

There followed one of the boldest military operations of the entire war. On May 20, 1941, exploiting their air superiority, the *Luftwaffe* launched

ONE-SIDED FIGHT

Germany's triumphs in Yugoslavia and Greece were overwhelming. The German army took prisoner 90,000 Yugoslavs, 270,000 Greeks, and 13,000 British and Commonwealth troops. The price Germany paid was about 5,000 men, killed or wounded.

an invasion of Crete by airborne troops who floated down by parachute or landed in gliders. British code breakers had provided precise information about enemy plans from intercepted messages, and German losses in the initial attack were heavy. But the Germans were allowed to seize control of an airfield at Maleme on northern Crete, after which they were able to fly in more troops and equipment in transport aircraft. By the end of May, 1941, the island was in German hands.

The British feared that the Germans might go on to capture other islands, especially Malta. Yet, although Malta was put under siege—hammered by continual *Luftwaffe* bombing raids and almost starved into submission as Germans sank ships that carried food and fuel to the island—it was never invaded.

Once Germany had attacked the Soviet Union in June 1941 (*see page 25*), Hitler viewed the Mediterranean as a sideshow. Rommel had to fight on

In the war in Yugoslavia, Axis soldiers conducted large-scale massacres of civilians, especially Serbs killed by the German, Italian, and Croatian troops.

General Bernard Montgomery was appointed commander of the British Eighth Army in North Africa in August 1942, three months before the victory at El Alamein.

THE BATTLE OF EL ALAMEIN

The forces engaged at El Alamein in October–November 1942:

Axis

men	104,000
tanks	489
artillery	1,219
aircraft	350

British Eighth Army

men	195,000
tanks	1,029
artillery	2,311
aircraft	530

Below: British infantry advance in the desert. Such "action" photos were almost always posed for the cameras.

in the North African desert with often inadequate resources. From the summer of 1941 to the summer of 1942, the fighting swung back and forth. Rommel's *Afrika Korps* generally won the tank battles, but he was never quite able to break through to Cairo and the Suez Canal in Egypt. His last offensive was stopped at Alam Halfa, in the Egyptian desert, in September 1942.

The war in the desert was far more important to Britain than to the Germans because it was at the time the only place where British troops dared engage the enemy in battle. The same logic dictated that the United States become involved in North Africa. In 1942 it was time for the U.S. Army, in the war since December 1941, to actively join the fight against Germany and Italy. The U.S. chiefs of staff favored an invasion of German-occupied France, but the British persuaded them that this was too risky. The United States then opted for an invasion of French North Africa to attack Rommel's forces from the rear.

EL ALAMEIN, EGYPT On October 23, 1942 the British Eighth Army, commanded by General Bernard Montgomery, launched a large-scale offensive against a well-prepared Axis defensive line at El Alamein, Egypt. By November 4, the British Eighth Army had broken through, forcing Rommel to retreat toward Tunisia. This victory was followed on November 8 by Operation Torch. Commanded by U.S. General

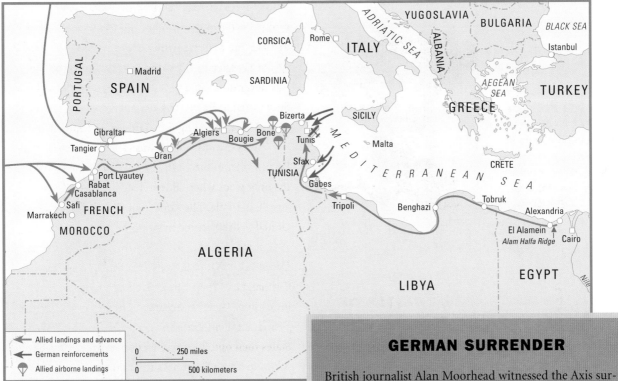

After its victory at El Alamein in October–November 1942, the British Eighth Army advanced across North Africa to Tunisia.

General Erwin Rommel was an inspired commander of German tanks in North Africa.

GERMAN SURRENDER

British journalist Alan Moorhead witnessed the Axis surrender in Tunisia. He wrote: *"We rode back . . . to Tunis, past the prisoners who now stretched in a procession reaching from the tip of Cap Bon far into Tunisia. Weeks were going to elapse before a final count revealed the total at over a quarter of a million prisoners . . . In all the Axis had lost close to a million men in Africa. Now they had nothing, absolutely nothing to show for it."*

—From *African Trilogy,* Alan Moorhead

Dwight D. Eisenhower, it landed Allied forces in French North Africa.

The last stages of the North African campaign did not go smoothly for the Allies. Unwilling to accept defeat anywhere, Hitler decided to give higher priority to the desert war and rushed reinforcements into Tunisia. Allied hopes that the Axis forces could be defeated by the end of 1942 were dashed. The troops that Hitler poured into North Africa, however, were sacrificed in a lost cause. Some 200,000 Germans and Italians were taken prisoner when their Axis forces surrendered in May 1943. The Allies could now use North Africa to launch an invasion of Italy.

CHAPTER 4
CLASH OF GIANTS

German troops advance through the ruins of a Russian village in July 1942. Hitler's order to carry a "war of annihilation" led the German invaders to devastate much of the Soviet Union.

After the Nazi-Soviet Pact of August 1939, Soviet dictator Josef Stalin behaved as a loyal ally of Hitler, supplying Germany with food and raw materials, including oil. As early as July 1940, however, Hitler informed his generals of his intention to invade the Soviet Union. Planning for the invasion, code-named Operation Barbarossa, began the following December.

Hitler felt contempt and hatred for the Soviet people, both because they were communists and because they were Slavs—regarded by Hitler as an inferior subhuman race. He told his generals that they were embarking on a "war of annihilation" (total destruction). Victory would, Hitler believed, make Germany unbeatable, with control of huge supplies of food and raw materials. There would be no country left in Europe capable of challenging German power.

The Germans had a low opinion of the Soviet Red Army, despite its huge size, and confidently expected to achieve total victory in one to three

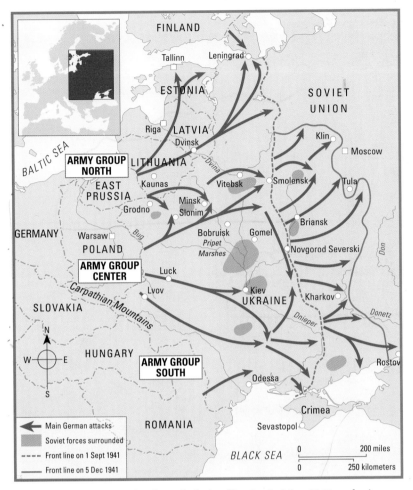

FINLAND
Tallinn — Leningrad
ESTONIA
SOVIET
UNION
Riga — LATVIA
Dvinsk
BALTIC SEA
Klin
ARMY GROUP
NORTH — LITHUANIA — Moscow
Dvina
EAST — Kaunas — Vitebsk — Smolensk — Tula
PRUSSIA
Minsk
Grodno — Slonim
GERMANY — Briansk
Warsaw — Bug — Bobruisk — Gomel
POLAND — Pripet — Novgorod Severski
Marshes
ARMY GROUP
CENTER — Luck
Lvov — Kiev — Kharkov — Don
Carpathian Mountains — UKRAINE
SLOVAKIA — Dnieper — Donetz
N
W E — HUNGARY — ARMY GROUP
SOUTH — Rostov
S — Odessa
Crimea
Main German attacks — ROMANIA — Sevastopol
Soviet forces surrounded — BLACK SEA — 0 — 200 miles
Front line on 1 Sept 1941 — 0 — 250 kilometers
Front line on 5 Dec 1941

Left: Invading the Soviet Union in June 1941, German forces advanced rapidly and captured millions of Soviet soldiers. Leningrad was put under siege, but the German advance ground to a halt in December without reaching Moscow.

Above: German soldiers found fighting in the Soviet Union much tougher than in earlier campaigns. They came to fear a posting to the Eastern Front as if it were a death sentence.

months. They intended to launch their offensive in May 1941 and win well before the dreaded Russian winter closed in. The start of Barbarossa was delayed, however, partly because the events in Yugoslavia and Greece required the Germans' attention in the spring (*see pages 20–21*). The launch of the offensive was finally set for June 22.

For the invasion, Germany assembled an army over three million strong along the border with the Soviet Union, from the Baltic in the north to the Black Sea in the south. It included not only Germans but also soldiers from Romania, Hungary, Italy, Finland, Slovakia, and Spain. Only a small part of this huge force consisted of armored divisions, however, and much of the army did not even have motorized transportation—there were 3,550 tanks involved in the offensive, but 700,000 horses.

Stalin received precise warnings of the coming offensive both from Britain, which was reading German coded messages, and from his own spies on his treacherous German partner, but he failed to call for full alert. As a result, his Soviet forces were taken by surprise, and their shallow defensive lines were easily broken.

The Soviets had more tanks and aircraft than their enemies, and

Soviet soldiers fiercely defended their homeland. Poorly organized, however, and poorly led, they faced total disaster the first month of the campaign. The German Army Group Center quickly advanced, taking Minsk and Smolensk by mid-July (*see page 25*). Had they continued, they might have taken the Soviet capital, Moscow. Instead, in August, Hitler ordered them to help Army Group South conquer the Ukraine. By the end of September, encircled Soviet forces in the south were forced to surrender at Kiev, while the German Army Group North waited outside Leningrad. By the time their advance on Moscow resumed at the beginning of October, however, the weather was already worsening. Heavy rains were followed by snow and bitter cold. By the end of November, the Germans were within about 12 miles (20 km) of the center of Moscow, but, without clothing or equipment for a winter war, they faltered in the face of dedicated Soviet resistance. On December 5, the Soviets forcefully counterattacked. Worn down by freezing cold and five hard

months of fighting, the Germans retreated for the first time in the entire war. Moscow was saved.

THE FATE OF LENINGRAD

Unquestionably, 1941 had been a catastrophic year for the Soviet armed forces. They had lost about a million men killed and 3.5 million taken prisoner. German losses had also been extremely heavy—about a million killed, wounded, or taken captive.

The suffering of the Soviet people was intense, especially in Leningrad, which was kept under blockade by the Germans for 900 days from September

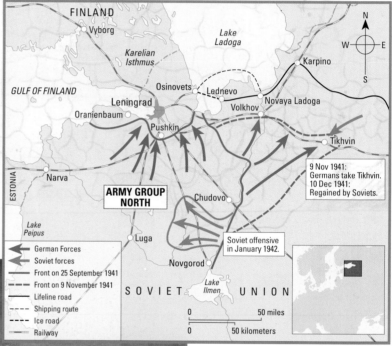

Above: Given the concentration of forces to the south, the only lifeline for supplies to besieged Leningrad was across Lake Ladoga, by boat in summer and by trucks across the ice in winter.

Left: This Soviet propaganda photograph shows snipers in snow camouflage fighting on the Leningrad front in 1943. Soviet troops generally were better prepared to fight in severe winter weather conditions than were their German enemies.

Cossack cavalry, from the Don region of the Soviet Union, ride out on patrol. Despite the use of tanks and trucks, horses played an important role in warfare on the Eastern Front.

OVERWHELMED BY DEATH

A Leningrad resident, Vera Inber, writing in her diary in December 1941, described how people were overwhelmed by the scale of the deaths in the besieged city: *"The mortuary itself is full. Not only are there too few trucks to go to the cemetery, but, more important, no gasoline to put in the trucks and the main thing is—there is not enough strength left in the living to bury the dead."*

—Quoted in *Russia's War*, Richard Overy

1941 to February 1944. The city's only lifeline to the outside world was across Lake Ladoga—bringing supplies by boat in summer and over the ice in winter. About a million of the Leningrad population died either under bombardment or of starvation and disease. The terrible brutality of German rule in the occupied areas ensured that, even among people who had suffered injustice and oppression under Stalin, there were very few who wanted to collaborate with the German invaders.

German artillery hits a factory in Stalingrad in 1942. Named after the Soviet dictator, the city became a prize neither side felt they could afford to lose.

The survival of the Soviet Union came as a huge relief to Britain and the United States, who desperately needed Stalin as an ally against Hitler. Stalin equally need the Western Allies, who provided a generous flow of modern military equipment, delivered to the Red Army via the Arctic port of Murmansk. In factories relocated to safety beyond the Ural mountains, the Soviets were also soon producing their own armaments in vast quantities, including tanks and aircraft that were a match for anything the Germans had.

In 1942, however, it still looked as if Hitler might win the war in the Soviet Union. In the first half of the year, the Soviets exhausted their strength in a series of costly and largely unsuccessful counterattacks. The Germans then launched a devastating offensive in the south that carried them to the Caucasus mountains, threatening the vital Baku oilfields. At the same time, the German Sixth Army advanced on Stalingrad, a city on the Volga River.

The Germans reached the suburbs of Stalingrad in mid-September, but the Soviets defended their city building by building and street by street. Two months later, elements of the Red Army were still holding out in the city, their backs to the river. On November 19, more Soviet forces counterattacked north and south of Stalingrad. They formed a noose around the city, with the German Sixth Army trapped inside and blocked from receiving supplies. All efforts to break the iron ring around Stalingrad failed. Despite an impressive effort to supply Hitler's Sixth Army by air in terrible weather conditions, the German troops ran short of food and ammunition. On January 31, 1943, German Sixth Army commander Field Marshal Friedrich Paulus finally surrendered.

A crushing defeat for Hitler, Stalingrad marked the turning point of the war. The Germans had reached the limits of their power. Now the forces against Hitler would only get stronger, as the Soviet Union and the United States focused their enormous reserves of manpower and industrial productivity on the war.

Left: In the summer of 1942, the Germans advanced to Stalingard and toward the important oil fields in the Caucasus. The Soviet counteroffensive in November cut off the German army and defeated them in Stalingrad, the turning point in the European theater of World War II.

Below: Of the 91,000 German soldiers taken prisoner by the Soviets in the battle of Stalingrad, most would die in captivity.

LOSSES AT STALINGRAD

Although Stalingrad was a defeat for the Germans, it is estimated that the more populous Soviets paid a higher price in casualties. They could afford such losses; the Germans could not. The majority of the German prisoners taken at Stalingrad died in captivity. German losses: 147,000 dead, 91,000 prisoners Soviet losses: about 500,000 dead

CHAPTER 5
OCCUPIED EUROPE

At the peak of its military success, Nazi Germany controlled a huge area of Europe from the Atlantic to the Caucasus Mountains and from Norway to the Mediterranean Sea. Every country on the European mainland except the Soviet Union had either been conquered, was allied with Germany, or was a neutral country that made itself useful to the Nazis.

Throughout German-occupied Europe there were shortages of food and other essentials of life. Here French people search through refuse in the hope of finding scraps to eat.

Below: At the end of 1942, Germany's domination of Europe was at its fullest extent. German troops had recently occupied Vichy France and pushed deep inside the Soviet Union.

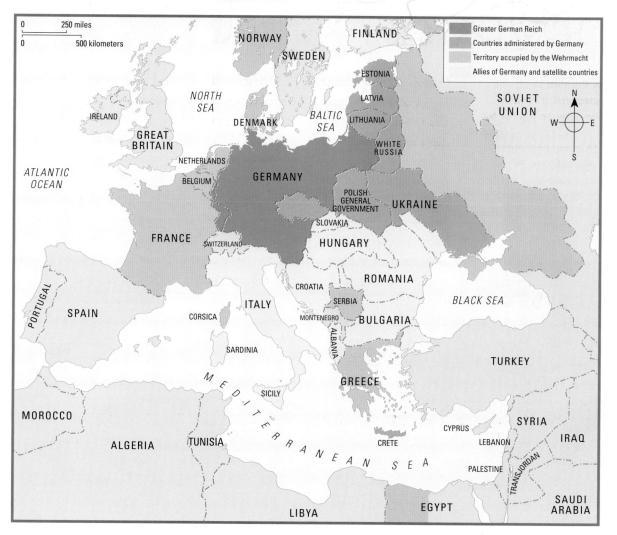

A German firing squad prepares a French Resistance fighter for execution. The Germans on many occasions executed groups of prisoners in retaliation for German officers or soldiers that had been killed by the Resistance.

In most countries that the Nazis occupied (Poland was a strong exception) they found political movements that were keen to imitate Nazi policies and that collaborated enthusiastically with the occupiers. The Vichy French government of Marshal Pétain, for example, actively collaborated with the Nazis even before the area of France it governed was occupied by the *Wehrmacht*, or German troops, at the end of 1942. Collaborators were often known as "Quislings," after the Norwegian Nazi leader Vidkun Quisling, head of government in Occupied Norway.

STARVATION AND NEGLECT
The scale of suffering under Nazi rule was almost unimaginable. Within Nazi-occupied Europe, many millions of people died in the course of the war—systematically or casually slaughtered by the Germans and their allies, or allowed to die of starvation or neglect.

The immediate demands of the war effort led the Germans to exploit conquered territories ever more intensely as the war became more desperate. For conquered peoples, this led to hardship and widespread malnutrition. Germany's growing labor shortage was met by forcibly importing hundreds of thousands of foreign workers and by using prisoners of war and inmates of concentration camps as slaves forced to work in factories and on building projects.

The way the Nazis behaved was also based on their long-term aim to create a "New Order" on the continent. The Nazi "New Order" was to be a Europe based on the domination of the so-called Aryan race—Germans and other blond, blue-eyed people—over the rest. The Slavs, regarded by Nazis as subhuman, were to be either reduced to slavery or exterminated to make room for German settlers in the east. The Poles (a Slav people) lost about one in five of their people in the course of the war. Soviet prisoners of war (also Slavs) died in the millions in German camps, and further millions of Soviet citizens perished during the occupation. The Roma and Sinti (Gypsy) people of Europe also suffered grievously under Nazi rule.

THE JEWS The only people treated worse than the Slavs were the Jews. German military successes brought about eight million Jewish people under Nazi rule. There was no room for them (or for Gypsies, homosexuals, or the mentally retarded) in the Nazi New Order. Europe was to be "cleansed" of Jews, regarded by Hitler as a demonic race responsible for Germany's and the world's ills. From 1941 onward, the Nazis embarked upon a "Final Solution" of the "Jewish problem." They set out systematically to exterminate the Jewish people—men, women, and children. At first, hundreds of thousands were killed by firing squad or gassed in the back of vans. Then death camps were established at sites inside occupied Poland—Majdanik, Chelmno, Treblinka, Sobibor, Belzec, Auschwitz— where they killed Jews in specially made gas chambers. The Nazis devoted massive resources to transport Jews from all over Europe to the death camps. It is estimated that about six million Jews were killed in this horrible effort, now known as the Holocaust.

The brutality of Nazi rule naturally led to resistance. Secret movements were set up in all occupied countries. Their activities ranged from organizing acts of passive resistance such as strikes or the concealment of Jews from their persecutors, to sabotage, assassinations, uprisings, and full-scale guerrilla warfare. The largest armed resistance movements were in the occupied areas of the Soviet Union and in Yugoslavia, where two mutually hostile guerrilla armies, one led by the communist Josip Broz Tito and the other by the Royalist Colonel Draza Mihailovic, fought the Germans, Italians, and Croats. Other substantial partisan groups included those in southern France and in northern Italy toward the end of the war.

Resistance movements pinned down considerable numbers of German troops that could have been used elsewhere in the war. In Poland, for example, when the underground Home Army staged an armed insurrection in Warsaw in 1944, more than 20,000

Above: Nazis used these ovens at the Dachau concentration camp in Germany to cremate the bodies of prisoners they killed.

Left: Jewish people deported to Auschwitz by the Germans under crowded cattle-car conditions wait to discover their fate. Many, including almost all children, were gassed to death within hours of arrival at Auschwitz.

German troops, backed by airpower, spent two months putting down the uprising. Although they tied up Nazi troops in this way, resistance groups were never strong enough to drive out the occupation forces unaided.

Britain tried to encourage resistance through the Special Operations Executive (SOE), set up in 1940, later helped by the American Office of Strategic Services (OSS). The SOE and OSS sent secret agents into Occupied Europe and also delivered arms and equipment to resistance groups. These perilous operations cost many brave people their lives but had limited effect.

As well as encouraging resistance movements, between

The Nazi camps dedicated to the extermination of Jews were located in the Polish General Government (German-occupied Poland). Concentration camps, used mostly to provide slave labor, were mainly in Germany. Auschwitz was both a concentration camp and an extermination camp.

SAVED BY SLAVERY

The lives of many Jews and Slavs were saved by the German need for slave labor in their factories, which led the Nazis reluctantly to keep them alive. Hitler's propaganda chief Joseph Goebbels wrote in his diary in March 1941: *"We have to go easy on the 30,000 Jews who work in armaments production; we need them—who would have thought this could ever become possible?"*

—Quoted in *The Holocaust*, R. G. Grant

A German soldier supervises the burial of massacred Polish Jews, probably in late 1941. The men digging would then also be killed.

1940 and 1943 the Western Allies carried out a few scattered coastal raids on German-occupied Europe. The largest of these, a landing at Dieppe, northern France, by Canadian troops in August 1942, was a disaster, with over 3,000 of the 5,000 troops involved either killed or taken prisoner.

THE BOMBING OFFENSIVE

There was one way, however, in which the Allies could strike at the very heart of Germany. This was through air attack. From 1940 onward, RAF Bomber Command carried out raids on Germany. In 1942, the

Legend:
- US bomber base
- Maximum range for B-17 and B-24
- Long range bombing
- Important strategic targets
- Neutral countries

Left: The scene in Hamburg, Germany, after bombing devastated the city in 1943. U.S. bombers attacked Germany by day and the RAF attacked by night.

Above: U.S. daylight bombing raids were at first launched from East Anglia in Britain. From 1943 onward, bases in North Africa and Italy brought targets such as the Ploesti oil fields in Romania within range.

PROFIT AND LOSS

The effectiveness of the Allied bombing campaign has been much disputed. Huge resources were devoted to it—the RAF alone dropped almost a million tons of bombs on Germany. The RAF and USAAF also paid a heavy price in lost lives. Yet, aside from the damage it caused, the bombing offensive forced the Germans to devote major resources to homeland defense—it occupied the cream of their air force. The death toll among bomber crews and civilians was:
RAF Bomber Command aircrew:
55,500 killed
USAAF Eighth Air Force aircrew: 26,000 killed
German civilians: 600,000 killed.

Airfield

U.S. B-24 Liberator bombers turn for home after raiding a German airfield.

U.S. Army Air Force (USAAF) joined in the bombing campaign. Based in eastern England, the USAAF carried out its bombing raids by day, depending on the firepower of its high-flying bombers to hold off German fighter aircraft. The RAF bombed by night, relying on the cover of darkness to get through the enemy defenses.

The bombing offensive was on a massive scale. In mid-1942, the RAF carried out raids with more than a thousand bombers in the sky at the same time. The night raids were often inaccurate and the bombers suffered heavy losses, but they could have a devastating effect on cities. In one night in July 1943, an RAF raid on Hamburg, Germany, is thought to have killed over 40,000 German civilians. Bombing by day, the USAAF sought to be more accurate, trying to hit specific factories or other economic or military targets. Bad weather and the intensity of German antiaircraft defenses meant, however, that the U.S. bombers also often missed their targets and paid a high price.

In August 1943, for example, the USAAF lost 60 bombers in a single day.

As the war went on, Allied bombing became increasingly effective. Allied advances in the Mediterranean meant that bombers were able to operate from North Africa and Italy as well as England. The introduction of the P-51 Mustang long-range fighter as a bomber escort in 1944 at last gave day bombers a real defense against German fighters. Improvements in navigation and tactics made even night bombers reasonably accurate. Although German factories never ceased to function, when the Allies bombed sources of fuel supplies, especially the Ploesti oil fields in Romania, they had a crippling effect on the German war machine in the last year of the war.

There was no let up in the air offensive as the war drew to a close. The Allied bombing of the city of Dresden, Germany, in February 1945 may have killed over 50,000 people. By then most German cities, including the capital, Berlin, had been reduced to ruins.

CHAPTER 6
THE TIDE TURNS

British troops wade ashore during the Allied invasion of Sicily in July 1943. The long hard fight up the Italian peninsula, which continued for the rest of the war, was launched from this point.

By 1943, Britain and the United States were eager to invade mainland Europe to create a "Second Front" that would bring relief to the Soviet Union, which was doing the bulk of the fighting against Germany. At a meeting held in Casablanca, Morocco, in January of that year, Roosevelt and Churchill chose Sicily as the target for their troops to reenter Europe— a much easier option than attempting landings on the north coast of occupied France.

North Africa was cleared of Axis forces in May 1943 (*see page 23*). The following July, Allied troops— American and British Commonwealth in almost equal numbers—crossed the Mediterranean. Since they had established supremacy both in the air and at sea, the Allies carried off the landings fairly smoothly, but they had to overcome some stubborn resistance from German forces on Sicily. The island was in Allied hands by mid-August.

The invasion of Sicily was the final blow to the prestige of Italian dictator Benito Mussolini. He was deposed and replaced by an Italian army officer, Marshal Pietro Badoglio. Although Badoglio assured the Germans that Italy would carry on fighting, he secretly sought peace with the Allies. An armistice between Italy and the Allies was announced in early September 1943, while the Allies invaded mainland Italy across the Straits of Messina from Sicily and by landing on the beaches at Salerno.

The Germans, commanded by Field Marshal Albert Kesselring, were swift to disarm Italian troops and take over the defense of the Italian peninsula. The Salerno landings were fiercely resisted by German *panzers*. Eventually forced to withdraw, the Germans pulled back in good order and stood firm along the Gustav Line, centered on the famous monastery of Monte Cassino. The advance of the Allied army—a multinational force including, among others, Poles, Indians, New Zealanders, and French North African troops—ground to a halt. Cassino did not fall until mid-May, three months after the monastery was bombed (*see box above*), and after intense fighting to clear a way for the Allied advance.

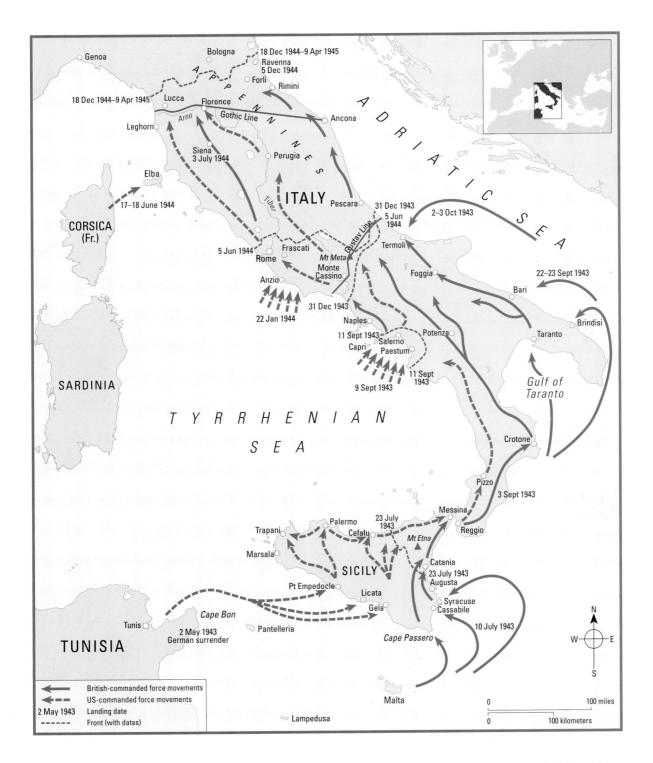

Genoa
Bologna
18 Dec 1944–9 Apr 1945
Ravenna
5 Dec 1944
Forli
Rimini
18 Dec 1944–9 Apr 1945
Lucca
Florence
Gothic Line
Ancona
Leghorn
Arno
A P P E N N I N E S
A D R I A T I C   S E A
Siena
3 July 1944
Perugia
Elba
ITALY
Tiber
Pescara
17–18 June 1944
31 Dec 1943
5 Jun 1944
2–3 Oct 1943
CORSICA
(Fr.)
5 Jun 1944
Frascati
Termoli
Gustav Line
Rome
Mt Meta
Foggia
22–23 Sept 1943
Monte
Cassino
Bari
Anzio
31 Dec 1943
Brindisi
22 Jan 1944
Naples
Potenza
Taranto
11 Sept 1943
Salerno
Capri
Paestum
SARDINIA
11 Sept
1943
Gulf of
Taranto
9 Sept 1943
T Y R R H E N I A N
Crotone
S E A
Pizzo
3 Sept 1943
Messina
23 July
1943
Palermo
Trapani
Cefalu
Reggio
Mt Etna
Marsala
SICILY
Catania
23 July 1943
Augusta
Pt Empedocle
Licata
Syracuse
Gela
Cassabile
10 July 1943
Cape Bon
Tunis
2 May 1943
Pantelleria
German surrender
Cape Passero
TUNISIA
Malta
Lampedusa

N
W — E
S

0   100 miles
0   100 kilometers

⟵ British-commanded force movements
⟵-- US-commanded force movements
2 May 1943 Landing date
------- Front (with dates)

THE "SOFT UNDERBELLY OF EUROPE" Trying to get
the advance moving again, the Allies landed a force at Anzio in January
1944, between the Gustav Line and Rome, but the Germans reacted swiftly
and hemmed them in. The Allies did not enter Rome until the next June—
and they still faced a further series of German defensive lines to the north.
Once described by Churchill as the "soft underbelly of Europe," Italy, now
controlled by Nazi Germany, proved to be a heavily defended adversary.

Allied occupation of Sicily and
then the invasion of mainland
Italy in September 1943 brought
hopes of swift progress. Instead,
their advance stalled in front of
Cassino. In spite of Anzio
landings in January 1944, the
Allies fought for two years to
reach northern Italy.

Left: Soviet *Katyusha* multiple rocket launchers prepare to fire during the Soviet counteroffensive against the German invaders. Fired in volleys, the rockets could deliver a devastating artillery barrage.

Below: Soviet troops advance through a Polish city in 1944. About one-fifth of the Polish population died during World War II.

Although the fighting in Italy was fierce, it was dwarfed by the scale and savagery of the conflict on the Eastern Front. There, the Soviet offensive of the winter of 1942–43, which had brought victory at Stalingrad, had carried the Red Army forward to a line that pushed west of the city of Kursk. In July 1943, the Germans launched an armored counterattack against the Kursk salient, hoping for a crushing victory that would once more give them the upper hand. But for the first time the German armor and its air support had met their match. In the largest armored battle ever seen, with more than 2,000 tanks committed on each side, the German offensive was repulsed and a Soviet counterattack forced the Germans to retreat.

BACK TOWARD GERMANY
From that point onward, the tide of war on the Eastern Front flowed in only one direction—back toward Germany. The Soviets now had tanks and aircraft as good as, or better than, those of the Germans, and their commanders used them with flair and intelligence. In September 1943, the Red Army reached the Dnieper River, and the following November they took the Ukrainian capital, Kiev. Soviet casualties were consistently much higher than those suffered by the Germans, but the Germans were increasingly outnumbered. About three million Axis troops faced more than six million Soviet soldiers at the end of

1943, and the Soviets had a similar superiority of numbers in tanks and aircraft—about twice as many as the Germans.

The siege of Leningrad was lifted in February 1944, and by May most of the Ukraine and Crimea were back in Soviet hands. The greatest remaining obstacle to the Red Army's advance was German Army Group Center, which continued to occupy Belorussia. In June 1944, the Soviets

Map legend:
— Front line at end of December 1942
Area occupied by Soviet forces by July 1943
Area occupied by Soviet forces by December 1943
Area occupied by Soviet forces by August 1944
Area occupied by Soviet forces by December 1944

SEEING THE ENEMY

Journalist Alexander Werth saw German prisoners paraded through Moscow in the summer of 1944. He described the reaction of the people who gathered to see their enemies in the flesh: *"The Moscow crowd was remarkably disciplined. They watched these Germans walk, or rather shuffle past, in their dirty green-grey uniforms. . . . I heard a little girl perched on her mother's shoulder say, 'Mummy, are these the people who killed Daddy?' And the mother hugged the child and wept."*
—Cited in the *Faber Book of Reportage*, John Carey, ed.

After the victory at Kursk in the summer of 1943, the Soviet Red Army drove the Germans out of the Soviet Union. In the center, their advance came to a halt just short of Warsaw, Poland.

launched Operation Bagration, a massive, complex offensive that in five weeks drove Army Group Center hundreds of miles back across the prewar Soviet border and well into Poland.

At the end of July, the Red Army in Poland stopped its advance on the east bank of the Vistula, the river that runs through the Polish capital, Warsaw. The Soviets, hoping to keep Poland for themselves, did nothing to help the Polish Home Army's uprising in the city (*see pages 32–33*), which was ferociously put down by the Nazis: more than 200,000 Polish civilians were killed. Instead, the Soviet advance continued further south. In the second half of 1944, Soviet forces invaded Romania, Hungary, and Yugoslavia, and reached the edges of Hungary's capital, Budapest, by the end of the year.

WORLD WAR II: EUROPE

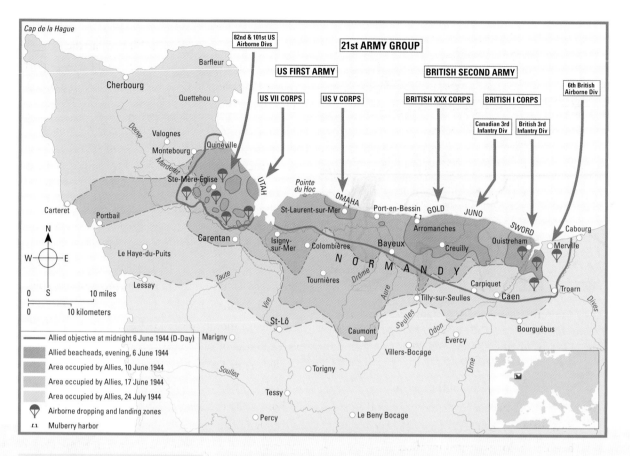

Cap de la Hague

82nd & 101st US Airborne Divs

21st ARMY GROUP

US FIRST ARMY

BRITISH SECOND ARMY

US VII CORPS

US V CORPS

BRITISH XXX CORPS

BRITISH I CORPS

6th British Airborne Div

Canadian 3rd Infantry Div

British 3rd Infantry Div

Barfleur

Cherbourg

Quettehou

Douve

Valognes

Montebourg

Quinéville

Carteret

Portbail

Merderet

Ste-Mère-Église

UTAH

Pointe du Hoc

OMAHA

GOLD

JUNO

SWORD

Cabourg

St-Laurent-sur-Mer

Port-en-Bessin

Arromanches

Ouistreham

Merville

N
W E
S

Carentan

Isigny-sur-Mer

Colombières

Bayeux

Creuilly

Le Haye-du-Puits

N O R M A N D Y

Carpiquet

Troarn

Taute

Tournières

Drôme

Tilly-sur-Seulles

Caen

Dives

0   10 miles
0   10 kilometers

Lessay

Vie

Aure

Seulles

Odon

Orne

St-Lô

Marigny

Caumont

Bourguébus

— Allied objective at midnight 6 June 1944 (D-Day)
   Allied beachheads, evening, 6 June 1944
   Area occupied by Allies, 10 June 1944
   Area occupied by Allies, 17 June 1944
   Area occupied by Allies, 24 July 1944
⛱ Airborne dropping and landing zones
🏠 Mulberry harbor

Torigny

Evercy

Villers-Bocage

Souloes

Tessy

Percy

Le Beny Bocage

D-DAY LANDINGS

Landing over 130,000 men on fortified beaches, the Allies expected heavier casualties on D-Day, June 6, 1944, than they actually suffered:

Troops landed
75,215 British and Canadian
57,500 U.S.

Casualties
4,300 British and Canadian
6,000 U.S.

Above: The beaches chosen for the D-Day landings were code-named Utah, Omaha, Gold, Juno, and Sword.

Below: American troops wade ashore on Omaha beach during the Normandy landings.

Allied Supreme Commander Dwight Eisenhower talking to men of the U.S. 101st Airborne Division before the Normandy D-Day landings.

The desperate situation of the Germans on their Eastern Front was matched by conditions in the West. On June 6, 1944—known as D-Day—the Western Allies began their long-awaited invasion of France with landings on the coast of Normandy. Carefully planned under the direction of Allied Supreme Commander U.S. General Dwight Eisenhower, Operation Overlord was the largest seaborne invasion ever launched, involving 1,200 warships, 5,000 landing craft and troop transports, and 10,000 aircraft. Two artificial harbors ("Mulberries") were towed across the Channel, so the army could be supplied and reinforced once ashore.

UTAH, OMAHA, GOLD, JUNO, AND
SWORD All the careful preparation was almost undone by the weather, which was so rough it seemed the invasion might have to be abandoned. Gambling on a brief break in the storms predicted by weather forecasters, however, Eisenhower embarked his U.S., British, and Canadian troops in southern England for a nighttime crossing to France. Airborne troops were dropped into Normandy under cover of darkness, and at dawn the seaborne troops landed on five beaches— code-named Utah, Omaha, Gold, Juno and Sword.

The invaders had some key advantages. Their command of the air and the sea was such that the

German air force and navy barely interfered. A clever Allied deception had convinced Hitler that the invasion would come in the area around Calais (a port around 155 miles [250 km] northeast along the coast), so that, even when news of the landings in Normandy came through, Hitler remained convinced that it was only a diversionary attack. Allied bombers destroyed communications links, making it difficult for the Nazis to swiftly order their reinforcements to Normandy.

Yet the success of the landings was hard won. The coast was heavily fortified. On Omaha beach, the American 1st Infantry Division suffered heavy casualties and was very nearly driven back into the sea. When a beachhead was established, progress was still slow. Montgomery's British and Canadian troops took more than a month to capture Caen, a town they had hoped to occupy on the first day of the invasion. The weather created problems: Low clouds blocked air operations and storms wrecked one of the Mulberry harbors in the third week of June. Capturing the port of Cherbourg at the end of the month was a step forward, but the failure to break through encircling German defenses meant that growing numbers of

A French woman takes a close look at a knocked out German tank in a Normandy town. The German *panzers* fought skillfully and tenaciously, but they were no match for an Allied air attack.

U.S. paratroopers advance as shells explode around them during Operation Market-Garden, in 1944.

Allied troops and quantities of supplies were bottled up in northwest Normandy.

In late July, while Canadian and British forces engaged the bulk of the German armored divisions, U.S. forces at last made the long-awaited breakout from Normandy, fanning west from Avranches into Brittany and east toward the Seine River. German troops launched a counterattack against Avranches, but suffered heavy losses. Canadian troops threatened to encircle the Germans from the north as they prepared to link up with Americans swinging up from the south near the town of Falaise. Many of the Germans managed to escape eastward before the "Falaise Gap" was closed on August 20, but now nothing could stop the Allies' rapid progress. On the same day, the spearhead of the U.S. forces crossed the Seine.

On August 15, a new front had been opened by Allied landings in Provence on France's Mediterranean coast. The French Resistance was in open armed revolt, taking on the German army in many parts of France, including Paris. A Free French armored division was allowed the honor of liberating the city on August 25, preparing the way for Free French leader General Charles de Gaulle to form a new government to replace the Nazi-collaborating Vichy regime.

SUMMER 1944   In the heady days of summer 1944, it was easy to imagine that the war in Europe would be over by the end of the year. Two million Allied troops, 60 percent of them from the U.S., were advancing on Germany from the west while the largest part of the German army was still forced to remain facing the Soviets in the east. Montgomery's British Second Army liberated the Belgian capital, Brussels, in the first week of September, by which time General George Patton's U.S. Third Army had reached the Moselle River, only 99 miles (160 km) from the Rhine River.

At this point, though, the Allies lost momentum. In Belgium, they captured the major port of Antwerp intact, with the help of the Belgian Resistance, but were unable to use it immediately because the Nazis

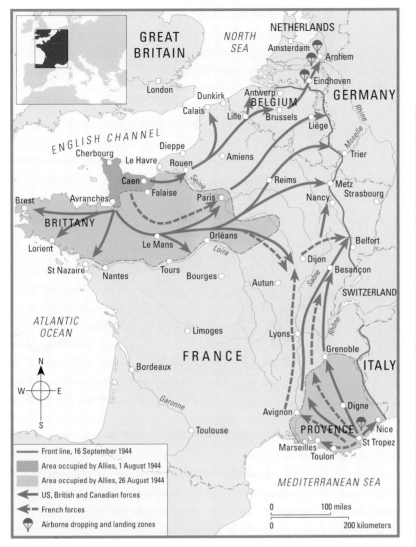

GERMAN WEAKNESS

It has often been debated whether a more vigorous offensive strategy could have allowed Allied troops to break through into Germany in the autumn of 1944. A German officer, General Westphal, wrote after the war: "*The overall situation in the West was serious in the extreme . . . Until the middle of October [1944] the enemy could have broken through at any point he liked with ease, and would have then been able to cross the Rhine and thrust deep into Germany almost unhindered.*"

—Quoted in *History of the Second World War*, B. H. Liddel Hart

remained in control of the Scheldt River leading into the port. Lacking river access to this port, the Allied armies struggled to get supplied from now distant Normandy ports, and their advance ground to a halt.

In a bold attempt to end the war quickly, on September 17, Montgomery launched Operation Market-Garden. Some 20,000 Allied airborne troops dropped into the occupied Netherlands by parachute and glider. They were to seize and hold a series of key bridges, allowing Allied tanks to drive across the Netherlands and into the Ruhr, Germany's industrial heartland. The final river crossing, however, at Arnhem, proved impossible. British paratroops could not hold it and the armored column failed to reach them in time. This failure condemned the Allies to continue fighting through the winter into 1945.

General De Gaulle, leader of the Free French forces, heads a parade along the Champs Elysées after the liberation of Paris in August 1944.

CHAPTER 7:
THE ROAD TO BERLIN

U.S. tanks struggle to cope with weather and road conditions in Belgium during the Battle of the Bulge, winter, 1944–1945.

By the summer of 1944, many senior German army officers were desperate to end the war before it resulted in the total destruction of their country. They led a plot to assassinate Hitler, overthrow the Nazi regime, and sue for peace. On July 20, 1944, the conspirators planted a time bomb at Hitler's headquarters in East Prussia. Although the explosion injured the dictator, he survived. Almost all those who had plotted against him were arrested and brutally executed.

It was far from certain that a non-Nazi German regime could have negotiated a peace deal, since the Allies had adopted a policy of "unconditional surrender"—meaning that the Germans must simply accept defeat and allow the victors to do with them as they pleased. It was certain, though, that with Hitler alive, peace was out of the question. Hitler would never agree to surrender, so the total conquest of Germany was the only sure path to end the war.

Faced with an apparently hopeless situation, Hitler put his faith in German "secret weapons" which entered the war in 1944. One of these, the first jet aircraft, had only a marginal effect on the conflict. In contrast, the

FAITH IN VICTORY

Hitler's generals felt that the December 1944 Ardennes offensive was absurdly over-ambitious. According to Field Marshal Gerd von Rundstedt, ordinary German soldiers did not share this scepticism: *"The morale of the troops taking part was astonishingly high at the start of the offensive. They really believed victory was possible —unlike the higher commanders, who knew the facts."*

—Quoted in *History of the Second World War,* B. H. Liddel Hart

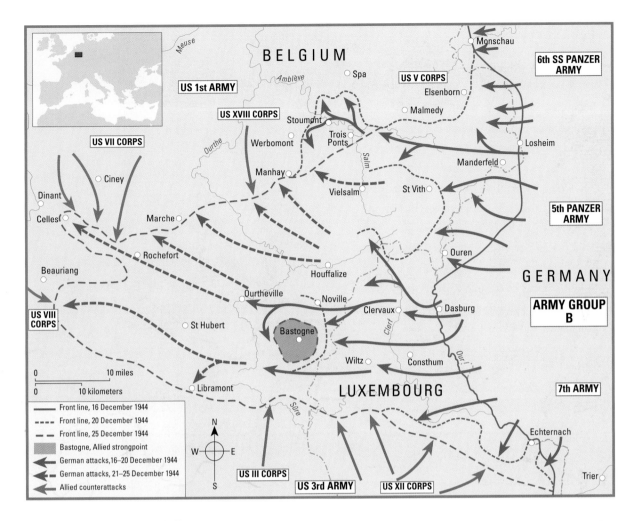

BELGIUM

6th SS PANZER ARMY

US 1st ARMY

Meuse

Amblève

Spa

US V CORPS

Monschau

Elsenborn

US XVIII CORPS

Stoumont

Trois Ponts

Malmedy

Loshem

US VII CORPS

Werbomont

Ourthe

Manhay

Salm

Manderfeld

Ciney

Vielsalm

St Vith

5th PANZER ARMY

Dinant

Celles

Marche

Rochefort

Ouren

Beauriang

Houffalize

GERMANY

St Hubert

Ourtheville

Noville

Clervaux

Dasburg

ARMY GROUP B

US VIII CORPS

Bastogne

Clerf

Wiltz

Consthum

Our

0   10 miles

0   10 kilometers

Libramont

LUXEMBOURG

Sûre

7th ARMY

Front line, 16 December 1944
Front line, 20 December 1944
Front line, 25 December 1944
Bastogne, Allied strongpoint
German attacks,16–20 December 1944
German attacks, 21–25 December 1944
Allied counterattacks

N
W   E
S

Echternach

US III CORPS

US 3rd ARMY

US XII CORPS

Trier

"V" weapons had much more impact on the war. The V-1 was a pilotless aircraft packed with explosives. The V-2 was the world's first supersonic ballistic missile—the forerunner of today's space rockets. Fired chiefly at London and Antwerp, the V-1s and V-2s together killed almost 9,000 people in England, but fell far short of having a decisive effect. For that they needed a nuclear warhead, as was finally used in the Pacific theater of World War II to end the war there.

ARMORED OFFENSIVE—BATTLE OF THE BULGE

Let down by his secret weapons, in December 1944 Hitler decided to gamble on a shock German counterattack. In virtually a repeat of May 1940, he ordered an armored offensive through the Ardennes region of Belgium. The tanks were to break through the Allied lines and advance rapidly across the Meuse River to the coast, taking the vital port of Antwerp, Belgium.

Launched on December 16, the Ardennes offensive (popularly known as the Battle of the Bulge) at first had just the success Hitler must have hoped for. The Ardennes front was thinly held by U.S. forces and

Above: The German offensive of winter 1944 is called the Battle of the Bulge because of how it pushed into Allied-held territory.

A V-1 pilotless aircraft, photographed over Britain in 1945. The V-1 would dive when its fuel ran out, exploding on contact with the ground.

surprise was complete. Allied aircraft, which could have countered the German advance, were grounded by severe winter weather.

The Americans, however, reacted swiftly. They rushed in reinforcements, tripling the U.S. forces in the Ardennes within four days. U.S. soldiers, especially those encircled at Bastogne, fought with great bravery. The German forces never reached the Meuse. On December 23, the weather lifted and Allied aircraft struck against the exposed enemy forces. On December 26, Patton's Third Army advanced from the south to relieve Bastogne (*see page 45*). By then German tanks and aircraft were running out of fuel. Through January 1945, in deep snow, the Germans made a fighting withdrawal back into their homeland. They had suffered about 100,000 casualties, and hundreds of aircraft and most of their tanks were destroyed. Hitler had made his last gamble and lost.

Hitler's only hope was that the Western Allies and the Soviet Union would quarrel. Instead, in February

NOBLE CRUSADE

The Allied advance revealed to the outside world the full horror of the Nazi death camps and concentration camps, with their medical experiments, gas chambers, and starving prisoners. For most people, this removed any doubts about whether the war was justified. British historian A.J.P. Taylor, who lived through World War II, wrote: "*No English soldier who rode with the tanks into liberated Belgium or saw the German murder camps at Dachau or Buchenwald could doubt that the war had been a noble crusade.*" —From *English History 1914-1945*, A. J. P. Taylor

1945, Roosevelt, Churchill, and Stalin, met at the Ukranian port of Yalta in Crimea (*see page 25*), and agreed on conquered Germany's immediate future.

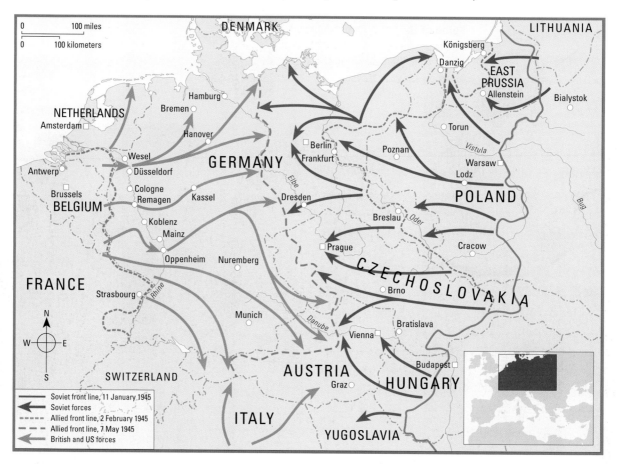

Germany was crushed between the Soviet forces advancing from the east and the Western Allies.

Hitler's last public appearance was in March 1945, when he distributed medals to members of the Hitler Youth movement.

On January 12, the Red Army launched a massive offensive from the Vistula River, where they had halted five months earlier. They conquered all before them, overrunning their prize, Poland, and crossing into Germany by the end of the month. Their spearhead was only about 39 miles (65 km) from Berlin. Further south, they conquered Budapest, Hungary, in mid-February, taking more than 100,000 German prisoners.

ON THE WESTERN FRONT

On the Western Front, Allied troops reached the banks of the Rhine in the first week in March. The Germans destroyed all the bridges across the river well in advance of the arrival of Allied forces, except at Remagen, where U.S. forces found a single bridge intact and crossed it on March 7. It was another two weeks before further Rhine crossings were made, by Patton in the south at Oppenheim and, shortly afterwards, by Montgomery in the north at Wesel.

Germany's situation was hopeless. Poorly armed members of the *Volkssturm*, Germany's Home Guard, were drafted into the front line to reinforce its vastly outnumbered and outgunned armies. German roads were crammed with refugees fleeing westwards in front of the advancing Soviet forces. Hitler, now installed in

Some of the 30,000 survivors of Dachau, where about 50,000 died, cheer their liberation by the U.S. Army on May 3, 1945.

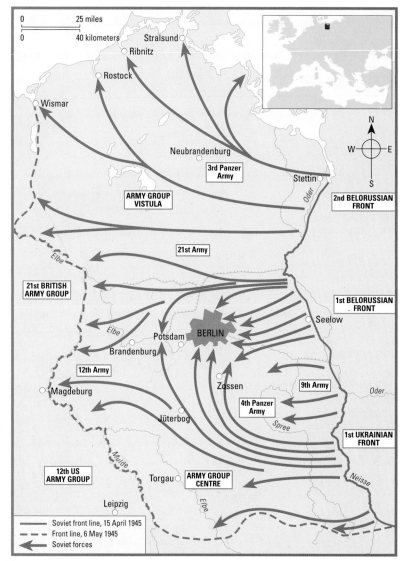

0 25 miles

0 40 kilometers

Stralsund
Ribnitz
Rostock
Wismar
Neubrandenburg

3rd Panzer Army

Stettin

ARMY GROUP VISTULA

2nd BELORUSSIAN FRONT

Elbe

21st Army

21st BRITISH ARMY GROUP

Elbe

1st BELORUSSIAN FRONT

Potsdam   BERLIN
Brandenburg

Seelow

12th Army

Magdeburg

Zossen

9th Army

Oder

Jüterbog

4th Panzer Army

Spree

1st UKRAINIAN FRONT

12th US ARMY GROUP

Torgau

ARMY GROUP CENTRE

Neisse

Leipzig

Elbe

Mulde

—— Soviet front line, 15 April 1945
- - - Front line, 6 May 1945
← Soviet forces

The First Belorussian Front, commanded by Marshal Zhukov, attacked Berlin directly from the east, while other Soviet forces joined in from south and north.

THE NATION WILL PERISH

Hitler was determined that if he was to go down, Germany would be destroyed with him. He gave orders to lay the country waste in the path of the invaders, saying: *"If the war is lost the German nation will perish. So there is no need to consider what the people require for continued existence."*

—Quoted in *History of the Second World War,* B. H. Liddel Hart

a bunker in Berlin, still hoped for some twist of fate. The Nazis seized upon President Roosevelt's death on April 12 as a miracle that might save their skins, but democratic transition went smoothly to Vice President Truman, and Allied policy did not change.

Avoiding a race with his Soviet ally, General Eisenhower decided to allow the Red Army to take the honor (and the heavy casualties) involved in capturing Berlin. Instead, the Western Allies mopped up in central Germany, accepting the surrender of more than 300,000 German soldiers in the Ruhr in mid-April. On April 25, Soviet and U.S. forces advancing from east and west met at Torgau on the Elbe River. By that time, troops commanded by Russian Marshal Georgi Zhukov were fighting their way into the Berlin

suburbs. Street-to-street battles raged, moving toward the heart of the city. On April 30, as the sound of gunfire shook his bunker, Hitler committed suicide.

Hitler's death did not immediately halt the fighting, which stuttered on until ended by a series of separate local surrenders. In Italy, Mussolini, who had been running a puppet government under German control since his fall from power, was captured by Italian partisans and shot on April 28. The following day, the German commanders in Italy signed an unconditional surrender. German forces in Berlin surrendered on May 2—taking the city that had cost the Soviets about 300,000 casualties. The armies in northwest Germany followed suit on May 4. Finally, on May 7, General Alfred Jodl signed a general unconditional surrender of all German forces, to take effect the following day. War in Europe was over.

WHEN THE FIGHTING STOPPED

Despite the enormous scale of World War II, it was not followed by any great peace conference setting out to redraw the map of Europe. When the leaders of the victorious Allies met at Potsdam, west of Berlin, in July 1945, the main item on the agenda was Japan, where World War II still raged. Most questions regarding Europe were either settled according to agreements that had been made in the course of the war or resolved by whoever was in military control of a given place when the fighting stopped. Much of eastern Europe was now therefore under Soviet control.

As they had agreed during the war, the Allies divided the defeated Germany into four occupation zones—American, British, French, and Soviet. Berlin was deep inside the Soviet zone, but it too was divided between the four Allied powers, each occupying a sector of the city. Austria, once more separated from Germany, was similarly divided into occupation zones.

The western border of the Soviet Union remained what it had become in 1941, so the Soviets kept the gains they made early in the war, including the Baltic Republics and eastern Poland. In compensation, Poland was allowed to take land from Germany in the west, shifting Poland westward. Czechoslovakia, Yugoslavia, Austria, and Hungary were broadly returned to the shape they had been given after World War I—the largest change was that Yugoslavia took Istria from Italy. Otherwise, changes of borders in Europe were small, although actual Soviet domination increased in many Eastern European countries.

Left: U.S. and Soviet troops meet at Torgau on the Elbe river on April 25, 1945. There was genuine warmth of feeling between soldiers of the Western Allies and their Soviet counterparts at this time.

Below: The Soviet flag is raised over the Reichstag building in Berlin, April 30, 1945.

Nazi leaders on trial at Nuremberg in September 1945.

IMPOSING A SYSTEM

During World War II Stalin told a fellow communist: *"This war is not as in the past. Whoever occupies a territory also imposes on it his own social system. Everyone imposes his own system as far as his army can reach. It cannot be otherwise."*

—Quoted in *Russia's War*, Richard Overy

In the years immediately after the war, much effort was put into the "de-Nazification" of Germany and the prosecution of Germans for war crimes (the Nuremberg Trials). The problem of German minorities outside the borders of Germany—the issue that Hitler had exploited so successfully in the 1930s—was settled crudely and brutally by driving them out of their homes. All the Sudeten Germans, for example, were expelled from Czechoslovakia. In total, some ten million German refugees, who had fled or been deported from lands to the east, had to make new lives for themselves in Germany.

Victory in the war had carried Soviet armies deep into the heart of Europe. They did not go home for more than forty years. The Soviet Union installed a repressive communist political and social system in the countries under its military control (Poland, Romania, Hungary, Bulgaria, and Czechoslovakia), while in Yugoslavia, the wartime resistance leader Tito also established a communist regime.

The United States, under President Harry S. Truman, was from 1947 committed to resisting the spread of communism worldwide. The U.S. took steps to prevent communist parties from taking power in Western Europe, including funding the Marshall Plan, a program to rebuild Western European economies and thus encourage social stability. In 1949, through the North Atlantic Treaty Organization (NATO), the United States pledged to defend Western Europe against attack by the Soviet Union. Like the Soviets, the U.S. forces had come to stay.

Because of the rift between the wartime allies, in Germany the military occupation zones solidified into a political divide. The U.S., British, and French zones became West Germany (the German Federal Republic) and the Russian zone became communist-ruled East Germany (the German Democratic Republic). West Berlin was left as a western outpost deep inside East Germany. The dividing line between communist-ruled Eastern Europe and the West was dubbed the "Iron Curtain." At the end of the 1980s and into the early 1990s, Soviet influence over Eastern Europe began to weaken. The Soviet Union itself broke up into Russia and other independent, noncomcommunist nations, and other Eastern European countries formerly under Soviet domination also turned toward democracy. Following the fall of the Berlin Wall in 1989, East and West Germany reunified.

The results of World War II were not entirely negative. Having experienced horror and destruction on a massive scale, Britain, France, Germany, and Italy were now motivated to bury their old differences and become partners in the European Union and NATO. A war between them became unthinkable. The people of Europe and their governments, it seems, truly did learn a lesson from history.

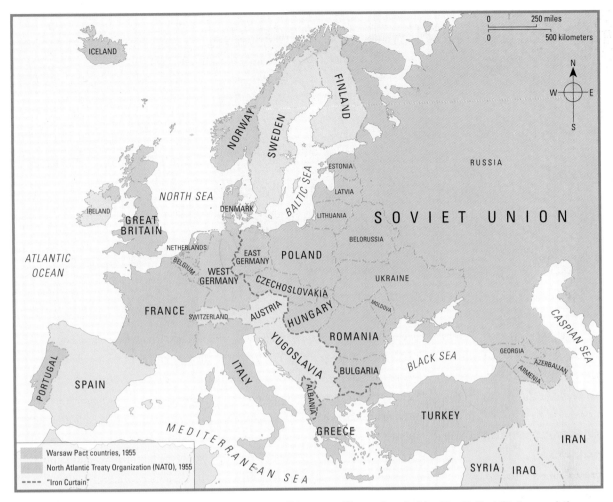

By the mid-1950s, Europe was divided between a Western alliance headed by the United States and the countries east of the Iron Curtain dominated by the USSR.

The Berlin Wall divided Berlin, Germany from 1961 to 1989, and was the most visible symbol of the division of Europe that followed World War II.

FIELD MARSHAL SIR HAROLD ALEXANDER (1891–1969)

Commander of the British rear guard, which held off the Germans during the evacuation of Dunkirk in June 1940, Alexander was the last British officer to leave France. In August 1942, he was appointed British Commander in Chief in the Middle East. He oversaw the victories in North Africa from El Alamein to Tunisia, the invasion of Sicily, and the Italian campaign. By the end of the war, Alexander was Allied Supreme Commander in the Mediterranean.

GENERAL OMAR BRADLEY (1893–1981)

After distinguishing himself as a corps commander in Tunisia and Sicily in 1943, Bradley commanded the U.S. forces at the D-Day landings in Normandy. During the campaign in Europe that followed, he commanded Twelfth U.S. Army Group. His swift decision making was to a large degree responsible for the defeat of the German Ardennes offensive in December 1944.

WINSTON CHURCHILL (1874–1965)

As a Member of British Parliament in the 1930s, Churchill led opposition to Prime Minister Neville Chamberlain's policy of appeasing Germany. He joined the government as First Lord of the Admiralty at the outbreak of war

and, in May 1940, replaced Chamberlain as prime minister, heading a coalition government including both Conservative and Labour politicians. In the summer of 1940, his policy of no surrender succeeded against defeatists in the government and his defiant speeches helped sustain British morale. He traveled widely during the war, at considerable personal risk, to maintain personal contact with Britain's Soviet and U.S. allies. Two months after victory in Europe, he was defeated in a general election.

GENERAL MARK CLARK (1896–1984)

Clark was U.S. deputy supreme commander under Eisenhower for the November 1942 landings in North Africa. He subsequently commanded the Fifth Army in the Italian campaign, from the Salerno landings in September 1943 to the German surrender in Italy at the end of April 1945.

GENERAL CHARLES DE GAULLE (1890–1970)

Before the war, de Gaulle was a French officer who vainly urged the French Army to modernize and adopt mobile warfare using tanks and aircraft. After losing the fight of May–June 1940 in France, he fled to Britain and established the Free French movement as a rallying point for those opposed to the pro-German French government at Vichy. When France was liberated in 1944, de Gaulle headed a provisional government. Largely as a result of his efforts, France was recognized as one of the victorious Allies in 1945, along with Britain, the U.S., and the Soviet Union.

ADMIRAL KARL DOENITZ (1891–1980)

Doenitz was appointed head of the German U-boat force in 1935. He masterminded the use of submarines in "wolf packs"— coordinated groups hunting down merchant ships. Commander in Chief of the German Navy from 1943, Doenitz was chosen by Hitler to succeed him as German head of state, a position he briefly held until arrested by the Allies in May 1945.

SIR HUGH DOWDING (1882–1970)

Commander in Chief of RAF Fighter Command from 1936, Dowding played a large part in organizing Britain's radar-based air defenses before the war. In May–June 1940, he resisted pressure to send too many RAF fighter aircraft to join the battle in France. During the Battle of Britain in July–September 1940, he made masterly use of limited numbers of men and aircraft to deny the *Luftwaffe* air supremacy.

GENERAL DWIGHT D. EISENHOWER (1890–1969)

Eisenhower was given command of the Allied invasion of French North Africa in November 1942. He proved so good at the difficult task of making British and American generals work together that he was made Supreme Commander for the Normandy landings in 1944. During the subsequent campaign in Europe, he was sometimes criticized for his cautious approach, preferring an advance on a broad front and refusing to race the Soviets to Berlin, which set up conditions for Soviet dominatation in the Cold War. After World War II, Eisenhower was elected to the U.S. presidency from 1953 to 1961.

REICH MARSHAL HERMANN GOERING (1893–1946)

An ace pilot in World War I, Goering joined Hitler's Nazi Party in its early days in 1922. A powerful figure in the Nazi regime after 1933, he took a special interest in building up the *Luftwaffe* (German air force). In 1940, he boasted that the *Luftwaffe* would bring Britain to its knees. The *Luftwaffe*'s failure dealt a crushing blow to his prestige. After the war, he was condemned to death at the Nuremberg War Crimes Trial but committed suicide before he could be executed.

GENERAL HEINZ GUDERIAN (1888–1954)

A leading tank expert in the 1930s, Guderian helped develop the *Blitzkrieg* style of fast-moving armored warfare. His *panzer* corps supported the German victory in France in May–June 1940. Guderian led the 2nd Panzer Group invasion of the Soviet Union, but he was fired by Hitler in December 1941 for military withdrawal against specific orders. Restored to favor, he was chief of the army general staff in 1944 when he again quarrelled with Hitler. He was on indefinite sick leave when the war ended.

AIR CHIEF MARSHAL SIR ARTHUR HARRIS (1892–1984)

Commander in Chief of RAF Bomber Command in 1942. He felt that bombing German cities would be a sure way to win the war if only enough resources were devoted to it. After the controversial bombing

of Dresden, Germany. in February 1945, he was criticized for having led a campaign that caused the deaths of hundreds of thousands of German civilians.

ADOLF HITLER (1889–1945)

Leader of the Nazi Party, Hitler became German Chancellor in 1933 and *Führer* ("leader") in 1935. By 1938, he had effectively achieved total control over the German officer corps. In World War II, he insisted on making major military decisions himself. The swift successes of the first years of the war confirmed Hitler's view of himself as an infallible Man of Destiny. His later mishandling of the war with the Soviet Union brought disaster on the German Army. After surviving an assassination attempt by German officers in July 1944, he killed himself on April 30, 1945, to prevent capture by the Allies.

FIELD MARSHAL ERICH VON MANSTEIN (1887–1973)

As a German staff officer in the winter of 1939–40, Manstein suggested a new strategy for the invasion of France, in which the main thrust would pass through the Ardennes instead of through northern Belgium. He won backing for this idea from Hitler. The brilliant success of Manstein's strategy was matched by his skill in the command of troops in the field, both in the defeat of France and subsequently in the invasion of the Soviet Union. In March 1944, Hitler fired him for retreating in the face of overwhelming Soviet forces. After the war, Manstein was charged with war crimes and spent four years in prison.

GENERAL OF THE ARMY GEORGE C. MARSHALL
(1880–1959)

Marshall was U.S. Army chief of staff from 1939 to 1945. He took up the post on the day the war in Europe began. He energetically pursued the expansion and modernization of the U.S. Army before the United States entered World War II in December 1941. Once the United States was at war, he consistently supported the view that the defeat of Germany had to be given priority over the war in the Pacific. He retired from the army in 1945 and became U.S. secretary of state from 1947 to 1949. During that time, he helped promote the recovery of Europe through the Marshall Plan. For this, he was awarded the Nobel Peace Prize in 1953.

FIELD MARSHAL SIR BERNARD MONTGOMERY
(1887–1976)

After performing creditably during the disastrous campaign in France

and Belgium in 1940, Montgomery was appointed to command the Eighth Army in North Africa in August 1942. The victory at El Alamein the following October made him a national hero. He fought in Sicily and Italy before becoming Allied Land Commander for the Normandy invasion in June 1944 and eventually leading Allied forces into northern Germany in 1945. A great believer in methodical planning and in crushing the enemy through superior forces, Montgomery was often criticized by U.S. generals for being slow and excessively cautious.

BENITO MUSSOLINI
(1883–1945)

As Italian dictator ("Il Duce") from the 1920s, Mussolini claimed to be recreating the glory of the ancient Roman Empire—but he was privately well aware of the weakness of his army and his country's economy. In June 1940, he declared war on Britain and France, hoping to sneak advantage from a war won by Germany. A string of military disasters led to his fall from power in July 1943. Rescued from prison by German

paratroops the following September, Mussolini was set up as head of a puppet Italian government in northern Italy. In April 1945, he was captured by Italian partisans and executed.

GENERAL GEORGE PATTON
(1885–1945)

America's most inspired commander of armored formations, Patton played a leading role in the fighting in Tunisia and Sicily in 1942–43. In 1944, he commanded the 3rd U.S. Army in Normandy and in the subsequent breakout across France. His swift response in December 1944 was crucial to the defeat of the German Ardennes offensive. A controversial figure, Patton nearly lost his command because of his aggressive attitude toward soldiers suffering from combat fatigue.

FIELD MARSHAL ERWIN ROMMEL (1891–1944)

Rommel performed impressively as a tank commander in the fighting in France in May–June 1940 and was promoted to head the newly formed *Afrika Korps* in February 1941. He generally out-thought and out fought the British in the Desert War—earning the nickname the "Desert Fox"—until the balance of forces turned overwhelmingly against him. Rommel had left North Africa by the time of the Axis surrender there in 1943. In command of the defense of northern France during the Normandy landings, he was badly wounded in an air attack on

his car. Rommel was then implicated in the plot to assassinate Hitler and killed himself rather than be arrested.

PRESIDENT FRANKLIN D. ROOSEVELT (1882–1945)

President of the United States from 1933, Roosevelt was publicly committed to keeping America out of World War II until his reelection to the presidency in November 1940. After that, he became increasingly open in his support for Britain. When the United States entered the war in December 1941, Roosevelt helped ensure that its major effort was directed against Germany, not Japan. Wartime summit meetings in which he took part included ones with Churchill

and Stalin at Teheran in 1943 and Yalta in February 1945. At these meetings the leaders agreed, among other things, that a defeated Germany would be divided into zones, each occupied by one of the victorious powers; and that Poland's borders would change, with the Soviet Union taking areas in the east and Poland being compensated with German territory in the west. Roosevelt died on April 12, 1945. After World War II ended, he was sometimes accused posthumously of having "delivered eastern Europe to communist domination," but there was probably little he could have done to prevent it.

JOSEPH STALIN (1879–1953)

Dictator of the Soviet Union, in the 1930s, Stalin was responsible for the deaths of tens of millions of Soviet citizens, including most of the Red Army officer corps, who were executed in a "purge" in 1937–38. His cynical non-aggression pact with Hitler in 1939, and his failure to prepare adequately for the German

invasion of 1941, brought his country to the brink of ruin. Yet between 1941 and 1945, he was able to motivate his people to heroic efforts through a mixture of patriotic enthusiasm and terror. Suspicious and cunning, Stalin mostly got the better of Churchill and Roosevelt in wartime meetings and he ended the war in control of eastern and central Europe.

JOSIP BROZ TITO (1892–1980)

Born Josip Broz, Tito was a Croatian communist who organized a band of partisan resistance fighters soon after the German occupation of Yugoslavia in 1941. He won the backing of Britain and the United States, who supplied his forces with arms and material, at the expense of rival partisans led by Draza Mihailovich. The Germans devoted some thirty divisions to the effort to suppress the partisans, but failed. After 1945, Tito and his Communist party ruled the Yugoslav Federal Republic.

MARSHAL GEORGI ZHUKOV (1896–1974)

An outstanding Soviet military commander, Zhukov won Stalin's confidence by leading first the successful defense of Leningrad against the Germans in September 1941 and then the defense of Moscow the following winter. He took much credit for surrounding the Germans at Stalingrad and for the Soviet victories of 1943 and 1944, and led the forces that captured Berlin in May 1945.

TIME LINE

MARCH 16, 1935
Germany announces that it rejects the disarmament clause of the Treaty of Versailles.

OCTOBER 3, 1935
Italy invades the independent African state of Abyssinia (now Ethiopia).

MARCH 7, 1936
German troops march into the demilitarized Rhineland.

JULY 17, 1936
The Spanish Civil War begins.

MARCH 12, 1938
German troops march into Austria; Austria becomes part of Germany (the *Anschluss*).

SEPTEMBER 29–30, 1938
The Munich agreement between France, Britain, Germany, and Italy forces Czechoslovakia to cede the Sudetenland to Germany.

MARCH 15, 1939
German troops occupy the Czech capital, Prague.

MARCH 29, 1939
General Franco, backed by Italy and Germany, wins the Spanish Civil War.

MARCH 31, 1939
Britain and France promise to come to the defense of Poland if it is attacked.

APRIL 7, 1939
Italy invades Albania.

AUGUST 23, 1939
The Nazi-Soviet Pact is signed, secretly providing that Poland will be divided between Germany and the Soviet Union.

SEPTEMBER 1, 1939
Germany invades Poland.

SEPTEMBER 3, 1939
Britain and France declare war on Germany.

SEPTEMBER 28, 1939
Invaded by the Soviet Union as well as Germany, Poland surrenders.

NOVEMBER 30, 1939
The Soviet Union invades Finland, starting the Winter War.

MARCH 12, 1940
The Winter War ends; Finland cedes some territory to the USSR.

APRIL 9, 1940
Germany invades Denmark and Norway.

MAY 10, 1940
Winston Churchill replaces Neville Chamberlain as British prime minister.

MAY 10, 1940
Germany invades the Netherlands, Belgium, and Luxembourg.

MAY 13, 1940
German tanks enter France through the Ardennes.

MAY 26–JUNE 3, 1940
Over 300,000 Allied troops are evacuated by sea from Dunkirk.

JUNE 10, 1940
Italy declares war on France and Britain.

JUNE 14, 1940
German troops enter Paris.

JUNE 22, 1940
France and Germany sign an armistice.

JULY–SEPTEMBER 1940
The Battle of Britain: the RAF defeats the *Luftwaffe's* efforts to establish air supremacy.

SEPTEMBER 1940
Beginning of the Blitz—the nighttime bombing of British cities (continues until May 1941).

NOVEMBER 11, 1940
British carrier-borne aircraft cripple the Italian fleet at Taranto.

FEBRUARY 11, 1941
General Erwin Rommel arrives in North Africa to command Axis forces in the Desert War.

MARCH 11, 1941
U.S. Congress approves the Lend-Lease Act to provide armaments to Britain.

APRIL 6, 1941
German forces invade Yugoslavia and Greece.

MAY 20, 1941
Germany launches an airborne invasion of the island of Crete.

JUNE 22, 1941
Germany invades the Soviet Union in Operation Barbarossa.

SEPTEMBER 8, 1941
Leningrad is cut off from the rest of the Soviet Union; it remains under siege until February 1944.

DECEMBER 5, 1941
Soviet forces launch a counterattack against the Germans in front of Moscow.

DECEMBER 7, 1941
Japan attacks the U.S. naval base at Pearl Harbor, Hawaii, forcing the U.S. into World War II.

DECEMBER 11, 1941
Hitler and Mussolini declare war on the United States.

MAY 30, 1942
The first 1,000-bomber raid against Germany is flown by British RAF Bomber Command.

AUGUST 19, 1942
Canadian troops raid Dieppe on the coast of occupied France and suffer heavy losses.

SEPTEMBER 13, 1942
The battle for Stalingrad begins.

OCTOBER 23–NOVEMBER 4, 1942
The (Second) Battle of El Alamein: British-led forces defeat Rommel's Axis forces and drive them into retreat.

NOVEMBER 8, 1942
In Operation Torch, U.S. and other Allied troops invade French North Africa.

JANUARY 31, 1943
Germans surrender at Stalingrad.

MARCH 13, 1943
German and Italian forces surrender in Tunisia.

JULY 5–14, 1943
The Soviet Union inflicts another defeat on Germany at the battle of Kursk.

JULY 10, 1943
Allied troops invade Sicily.

JULY 25, 1943
Mussolini is deposed as Italian head of government.

JULY 27–28, 1943
An RAF bombing raid on Hamburg kills about 40,000 people.

AUGUST 17, 1943
Sixty U.S. bombers are shot down during raids on German factories.

SEPTEMBER 8, 1943
The Italian surrender is announced; Allied troops land at Salerno the following day.

NOVEMBER 6, 1943
The Soviet army recaptures the Ukrainian capital, Kiev.

JANUARY 22, 1944
Allied forces land at Anzio, south of Rome.

MAY 18, 1944
Allied troops in Italy finally break through the Gustav Line at Monte Cassino.

JUNE 4, 1944
Allied forces enter Rome.

JUNE 6, 1944
D-Day: Allied forces land on the beaches at Normandy, beginning the invasion of France.

JUNE 21, 1944
The Soviets launch Operation Bagration, a major offensive that drives the Germans back into Poland.

JULY 20, 1944
An attempt by German officers to assassinate Hitler fails.

AUGUST 1, 1944
The Polish Home Army launches an uprising against the Germans in Warsaw.

AUGUST 1, 1944
U.S. forces in Normandy break through at Avranches.

AUGUST 24, 1944
Paris is liberated.

SEPTEMBER 3, 1944
Brussels, Belgium, is liberated.

SEPTEMBER 17, 1944
Allied airborne troops are dropped into the Netherlands in Operation Market-Garden.

DECEMBER 16, 1944
The Germans launch a surprise counterattack in the Ardennes, beginning the Battle of the Bulge.

JANUARY 12–31, 1945
The Soviets resume their offensive from the Vistula and push into eastern Germany.

FEBRUARY 4–11, 1945
Stalin, Roosevelt, and Churchill meet at Yalta.

FEBRUARY 13, 1945
Soviet troops capture Budapest, Hungary, after a lengthy siege.

FEBRUARY 13–14, 1945
Allied bombers destroy the city of Dresden, Germany.

MARCH 7, 1945
U.S. troops cross the Rhine River at Remagen, Germany.

APRIL 12, 1945
Roosevelt dies; Harry S. Truman becomes president.

APRIL 28, 1945
Mussolini is killed by Italian partisans.

APRIL 25, 1945
Soviet and U.S. troops meet at Torgau, Germany, on the Elbe River.

APRIL 30, 1945
Hitler commits suicide in his Berlin bunker.

MAY 2, 1945
Berlin falls to the Soviet army.

MAY 7, 1945
German commanders sign a general surrender.

MAY 8, 1945
VE (Victory in Europe) Day.

GLOSSARY

airborne troops Soldiers carried into battle by air, usually parachuting to the ground.

annex To add territory to a country by occupying or conquering it.

appeasers Term used for British and French political leaders of the 1930s who believed that making concessions to Hitler would ensure peace.

armistice An agreement to stop fighting.

armor In modern warfare, a term for fighting vehicles such as tanks that are protected by metal plates.

armored columns Large formations of tanks and other armored fighting vehicles.

Aryan race According to racist theories embraced by the Nazis, a superior race of human beings, of which Germans were part, that excluded Jews, Gypsies, Slavs, and other groups.

beachhead An area on an enemy beach or shoreline captured by an invasion force, where more troops and supplies can be landed.

blitzkrieg In German, literally "lightning war"——a fast-moving offensive, especially using tanks and aircraft, designed to deliver a knockout blow to the enemy as rapidly as possible.

coalition Term for a government made up of representatives of more than one political party.

collaborate In Nazi-occupied Europe, to cooperate with the Nazis and help implement their policies.

colonial authorities People running a foreign country as a colony or some other territory as part of their own country's empire.

Commonwealth troops Soldiers from one of the independent states once ruled by Britain, including Australia, New Zealand, Canada, and South Africa.

communism Political and economic system of the Soviet Union, which spread to other countries after 1945. It favors a classless society and common ownership of property and means of production.

demilitarized Indicating a place where no military forces are allowed to be stationed.

democratic Having a government that is elected by the people and that allows a diversity of political movements and opinions.

disarmament Giving up some or all of one's weapons, usually by agreement between countries.

expeditionary force A term used in both World War I and World War II for the British troops sent to France at the start of the war.

front A place where hostile armies confront one another in a theater of war.

guerrilla war War waged by irregular troops of a patriotic or revolutionary movement that employ tactics of surprise attack and harassment against an occupying or advancing enemy.

Lend-lease program System by which the United States provided weapons and other supplies to its Allies in World War II without requiring immediate payment for them.

minorities Groups that differ in some way from the majority of the population in the society or country of which they are part.

mobilize To set in motion preparations for going to war.

Nazism A system of government in Germany from 1933 to 1945 based on a belief in racial superiority and the rule of a strong and ruthless leader.

neutral countries Countries that do not take part in a war or give support to one of the warring sides.

OSS The acronym for the Office of Strategic Services, set up by the United States in 1942 to gather intelligence and carry out secret operations.

panzers German tanks and other armored vehicles.

partisans Irregular troops fighting a guerrilla war.

partition The division of a country or area into different parts.

patriotic Referring to someone who is loyal to and supports his or her own country.

propaganda Information, often false or exaggerated, that is deliberately intended to promote a particular cause or to damage an enemy.

puppet government A government controlled by another power.

regime System of government; also a particular government or administration.

resistance movements Groups organized to oppose the government or foreign occupation forces in their country.

rout a disorderly retreat from a victorious enemy.

sabotage The deliberate destruction of material, such as fuel, roads or bridges, to thwart the plans of an enemy.

salient Part of the front line that pokes forward into enemy-held territory and so is surrounded by the enemy on three sides.

Slavs Inhabitants of countries in Eastern Europe, including Russia, Ukraine, Belorussia, Poland, Czechoslovakia, Bulgaria, and Yugoslavia, who speak languages from the Slavic language group.

SOE Acronym for the Special Operations Executive, an organization set up by Britain in 1940 to send secret agents into enemy-occupied Europe.

SS Acronym for *Schutzstaffeln*, an elite unit in the Nazi party, which also had its own armed troops—the *Waffen* SS.

theater of war A geographical area in which part of a war is fought—for example, "the Mediterranean theater."

unconditional surrender The policy of the Allies, who decided that there would be no peace negotiations with their enemies; the enemy countries could not ask for any special conditions for their surrender.

Vichy France After Germany's defeat of France in June 1940, the French government that cooperated with Nazi Germany moved from Paris to the town of Vichy. The area of southern France that this government ruled, called Vichy France, was aligned with Nazi Germany.

Wehrmacht The German armed forces.

wolf packs Groups of German submarines hunting together for ships to sink in the Atlantic.

STATISTICS CONCERNING COMBATANT NATIONS

Casualties

Australia
A total of 9,572 military dead, excluding the war against Japan, including:

Navy	903
Army	3,552
Air Force	5,117

A total of 27,073 military dead, including the war against Japan.

Britain

Military killed:	total: 264,443
	Navy: 50,758
	Army: 144,079
	RAF: 69,606
Civilians killed:	62,974
Merchant seamen killed:	29,180

Canada

military killed:	total: 42,042
	Navy: 2,024
	Army: 22,917
	Air Force: 17,101
Merchant navy killed:	1,148

France

Military killed:	210,000 (of which 40,000 from Alsace-Lorraine fighting for Germany)
Civilians killed:	150,000 (bombings and resistance fighting)
Prisoners and deportees:	240,000

Germany
Total military deaths: 3,712,888
Military killed and missing (to January 1945)

	Navy: 149,160
	Army: 3,269,000
	Air Force: 294,728
Civilian dead:	780,000 (estimate)

Italy
An estimated 150,000 army dead (including fighting for Allies); 50,000 naval and air deaths; perhaps 100,000 civilians died as partisans, in bombing, or after being deported

India (including present-day Pakistan and Bangladesh)
Total: 36,092 killed, mostly fighting against Japan.

New Zealand

War deaths total:	11,671
Navy:	573
Army:	6,839
Air Force:	4,149
Merchant Navy:	110

South Africa
War deaths: total about 9,000, including Air Force deaths: 2,227

Soviet Union
military killed: total: 8,668,400
(including 3.3 million who died as prisoners of war)
Civilians killed: 17 million (lowest estimate)

United States of America
Total U.S. dead (all theaters of war):

Total dead:	405,399
U.S. Navy:	62,614
U.S. Army:	318,274
U.S. Marines:	24,511

Other European Death Tolls (estimates)

	military	civilian
Belgium:	12,000	76,000
Czechoslovakia:	10,000	215,000
Denmark:	1,800	2,000
Finland:	82,000	2,000
Greece:	79,743	350,000
Hungary:	200,000	290,000
Netherlands:	7,900	200,000
Norway:	3,000	7,000
Poland:	123,000	5,675,000
Romania:	300,000	200,000
Yugoslavia:	305,000	1,200,000
Jews:		6,000,000
Gypsies:		200,000–600,000

RECOMMENDED BOOKS

The following books look at World War II and focus on the war in Europe:

Adams, Simon. *Eyewitness World War II.* DK Publishing, 2000.

Ambrose, Stephen E. *Citizen Soldiers: The U.S. Army from the Normandy Beaches to the Bulge to the Surrender of Germany, June 7, 1944—May 7, 1945.* Simon and Schuster, 1997.

Anflick, Charles. *Teen Partisans and Resisters Who Fought Nazi Tyranny.* Rosen Publishing Group, 1999.

Gottfried, Ted. *The Great Fatherland War: The Soviet Union in World War II.* Milbrook Press, 2003.

Panchyk, Richard. *World War II for Kids: A History with 21 Activities.* Chicago Review Press, 2002.

Patterson, Don. *Scramble! Tales of the RAF.* Hindsight Limited, 1999.

Schomp, Virginia. *World War II.* Benchmark, 2003

Stein, R. Conrad. *World War II in Europe.* Enslow, 2003.

Verhoeven, Ryan, and Ruud Van der Rol. *Anne Frank Beyond the Diary: A Photographic Remembrance.* Puffin, 1995.

Warren, Andrea. *Surviving Hitler: A Boy in the Nazi Death Camps.* HarperCollins Publishers, 2002.

RECOMMENDED VIDEOS

The following videos are available on VHS or DVD:

World War II: When Lions Roared (1994)

The Air Power Collection (2002):
> Volume 1: *The Nazi War Machine*
> Volume 2: *Allied Victory*

People's Century: the Saga of World War II Series (1999): *Master Race: Nazism Overtakes Germany*

World War II: The Leaders—Vol. 2 (1998)

Total War: World War II and the Home Front (1999)

RECOMMENDED WEBSITES

The Internet offers a vast archive of material both on the war in general and on every aspect of it. Starting points on the web might be:

www.historyplace.com/worldwar2
www.worldwar-2.net
World War historylacusd.edu/gen/ww2_links.html

Note to parents and teachers

Every effort has been made by the publishers to ensure that these web sites are suitable for children; that they are of the highest educational value; and that they contain no inappropriate or offensive material. However, because of the nature of the Internet, it is impossible to guarantee that the contents of these sites will not be altered. We strongly advise that a responsible adult supervise Internet access.

PLACES TO VISIT

Among places to visit connected to the war in Europe, top of the list must be the Normandy beaches. Apart from the beaches themselves, Normandy is dotted with World War II cemeteries and museums. Some U.S. museums partly or totally devoted to the war are:

The Naval Historical Center, Washington Naval Yard, Washington, D.C. 20374 (*www.history.navy.mil*)
The National World War II Memorial in Washington, D.C. (*www.wwiimemorial.com*)
U.S. Air Force Museum, Dayton, Ohio (*www.wpafb.af.mil/museum/index.htm*)

ABOUT THE AUTHOR

The author, Reg Grant, studied history at the University of Oxford and is the author of more than a dozen books on modern history. He specializes in the history of the twentieth century. His book *The Holocaust* (1997) was shortlisted for the *Times Educational Supplement*'s Senior Information Book Award.

Numbers in **bold** refer to captions to pictures or, where indicated, to maps.